EXTRAORDINARY WOMEN: HELPING A SISTER OUT

Evaleen Litman Talton Sargent, M.Div.

EXTRAORDINARY WOMEN: HELPING A SISTER OUT

Evaleen Litman Talton Sargent, M.Div.

Copies of this book are available from:

Rev. Evaleen Litman Talton Sargent, M.Div.
ELS Ministries
P.O. Box 311859
Atlanta, Georgia 31131-1859
(404) 691-0636 / (404) 316-6862
E-mail: elsministries@bellsouth.net

PUBLISHED BY:
BRENTWOOD CHRISTIAN PRESS
4000 BEALLWOOD AVENUE
COLUMBUS, GEORGIA 31904

About this Book

This book is written by and for the woman who believes it would be in her best interest to walk through the torn curtains of the temple and into the Holy of Holies where you have direct access to God. It is also for the woman who is now willing to lay herself at the foot of the altar of the Lord, baring all before her Creator, Sustainer and her Lord. Realizing that after all is felt, said, heard and done, she will be a new creation in Christ. She will be uninhibited and able to live out her true passion and divine purpose (eternal destiny).

These chapters contain insights into the lives of women that will aid men in understanding the ongoing intimate love-relationship between God and woman. As you read this work you will feel the vibrancy, passion, abandonment, disappointment, fury, struggle, contrition, and exuberant joy of being a woman who has been awaken to her true self. Then you will celebrate with these women as most of them are blessed, healed, delivered, reconciled, restored, and resurrected to a right relationship with the Lord.

Dedication

I humbly offer this endeavor to the reconciling work of the Holy Spirit within us. And I dedicate this book to my sons, the Reverend Delvin D. Talton, Sr. and the Reverend James E. Talton, II, whose lives were dedicated to God for divine purposes before they were conceived and as they grew in my womb. It is partially because God blessed me to be their mother that I am the person I am this day. May the words found herein aid your understanding and spiritual love of your wives, daughters, co-laborers in ministry and the women in the pews. This work is also dedicated to my beautiful daughters-in-law and grandchildren, my mother, siblings and their families, and my special daughter and son-in-law and family. I thank each of you for your prayers, encouragement and support.

I dedicate this book to my family, but over the years, many persons have encouraged me to write a book or to publish my autobiography. There are countless persons who have recognized and affirmed God's call on my life; my dear friend and daughter in the ministry, the Reverend Yvette D. Massey, Mrs. Alberta Martin, Mrs. Ardella Stabler Jennings, Mrs. Vicki Callaway, Mrs. Annie B. Mahone, Mrs. Ruby McGregor-Bibbs (deceased), Mrs. Teresa Sutton, Mrs. Linda D. Strickland, Mrs. Catherine Holt, Mrs. Carole Reese Taylor, Pastor Paula Christian-Stallworth, the Reverend Elizabeth Godfrey, Minister Karen Kelley, Mrs. Minnie Friendly (deceased), Mrs. Gwendolyn Hurston, Dr. Betty Jones, the Reverend Kathi R. Chavous, Mrs. Joan N. Branch, Deaconess Lucindy Walker, Mrs. Joann W. Scott, Mothers Betty Jones and Rosetta Smith, members of the Atlanta Baptist Association, New Era Convention and Congress,

Progressive National Baptist Convention, American Baptist Churches of the South and U.S.A., my Pastor, fellow Associate Ministers, church school class and my present and past church families, my big-little brother and every pastor and congregation who has opened their pulpit to me – you have been a great source of encouragement and motivation for my ministry and my writing projects. May God continue to fan the flames of my role models in the ministry: Dr. Lorraine Jacque White, Bishop (Dr.) Rosa L. Williams, Dr. Ella Pearson Mitchell, and the late Dr. Charles Jackson Sargent. And I can never forget Dr. Tim, my personal counselor, and my faithful neighbors: Bernice, Larry, Jackie and their families.

This list is incomplete. God knows the love that you have extended and the opportunities that you have given me to utilize my gifts. Your telephone calls, kind words, cards, notes, movies, meals, donations and love continue to be a blessing, and your prayers for me are being answered daily. To every person who has ever touched my life, I am...because you allowed God to use YOU! I thank you from the depths of my soul for "Helping a Sister Out."

Contents

Introduction

Although some of the insights that I will share were inspired by God over a span of forty years (I was a slow learner.), the written work began to take form on Friday, August 29, 2003 during the mid-point of a sabbatical from my home church. This period of prayer and meditation was called "My Forty-Day Journey of Intimacy with God." It involved solitude, studying scripture, maintaining a proper diet, exercise, social and cultural experiences, getting enough rest, and directed prayer. For many people, these disciplines are a part of their daily life, for me this required great effort. I was praying to God about my divine purpose in life, after twenty days God finally began to speak.

It was during the latter days of this forty-day journey that I felt a need to draw closer to God. I had reached a point in my life and ministry when I was no longer sure of my divine purpose in life. I had used my secular work and my ministry to God's people to cover over a lot of hurt, disappointment and unfulfilled longings. I was becoming disillusioned with game playing church folks who used the name of God to oppress God's people and God's anointed. I was having a "crisis of the soul." I was ready for healing from the inside out. I wanted to remove anything that was separating me from God and God's purpose - from my life. I wanted to be restored to a right relationship with the Lord who had called me out of darkness and into the marvelous light. I also wanted to be resurrected in body, mind and spirit.

Healing as it is referred to here is to cause an undesirable condition to be overcome. It can range from poor health to any form of illness to a breach between friends. Deliverance is to be set free. It involves liberation and rescue from those beliefs, traditions, biases and people preventing you from experiencing the fullness of God and life's awesome possibilities. Restoration is the return to and/or reconciliation with God. In restoration, you are placed back in God's possession. Resurrection is a revival of spiritual understanding. It has to do with the efficacy of Christ's resurrection in the life of a believer. It is a new beginning. Not starting where you left off but starting afresh. Resurrection is starting afresh at the point where you are. In resurrection you die to your old life and problems. In resurrection you shake the dust off your feet and rise above mediocrity. In resurrection, you live out your new life in Christ in the world where you are without being crushed in the press or being consumed by swine. At other times it is a matter of making peace with your life and then you move on to better days ahead. In resurrection, you attain God's best for your life. When you find healing, deliverance, restoration and resurrection in your relationship with God, they will have a direct affect on your relationship with others. Then you are free to live out your divine purpose.

During the later part of my journey of intimacy with God, the Lord had me revisit many life experiences that had long since been forgotten. I kept a journal of the entire forty-day journey. This journal was separate from my notes for this book. During my journey, I learned that creative inspirational writing is a large part of my divine purpose in life.

In writing this book, I felt a lot like Paul must have felt when he described his abilities in his first letter to the church at Corinth. I write "not with eloquent wisdom, so that the cross of Christ might not be emptied of its power."[1] This book is written for women from diverse backgrounds and women of different stations in life. The language moves from simple words to the theological terminology that is explained in footnotes. I write under the unction of the Holy Spirit so that God may be more fully revealed to a waiting world. This work is written for the churched and unchurched. "So that which had not been told them they shall see and that which they had not heard they shall contemplate."[2] I have also used extra-biblical literature, scholarly references, and proven mother-wit so that I do not mislead anyone with clichés and mindless babble. Any likeness of any situation or character to yourself is God's revelation to you. Any likeness of any situation or character to someone that you may know is for your insight into understanding and loving that sister, more.

From the outset, when God gave me the vision to write a book for women, God gave me the thirteen names of the women that I was to write about. They were Martha, Mary, her younger sister, Athaliah, Deborah, Jephthah's daughter, A Crippled Woman, The Woman with an Issue of Blood, Tabitha, more commonly known as Dorcas, Rahab, Euodia and Syntyche as one, Mary Magdalene, Eve, and Me (as an unwritten book). The one thing that I could not understand was why God had me write my name, at the end of the list, as one of those women. My name is not in the canon. As I inquired of the Lord, God was silent. It was not until the book was complete that I understood what God had done. This book has become a part of my own personal journey of healing, deliverance, restoration and resurrection. God wanted me to share parts of my own personal story of 'the movement of the Holy Spirit across the altar of my soul' in order that I might help another sister with her journey to wholeness.

Extraordinary Women: Helping a Sister Out was to be the title. Although God gave me the title, the words 'extraordinary women' go back to a bouquet of flowers that my brother in-law, Luther and my youngest sister, Addie sent to me several years ago when I was ending one phase of my life and beginning a new one. Their card read, "12 roses are for ordinary people, 13 are for extraordinary people." Throughout biblical history God has used ordinary or unlikely people to do God's extraordinary work.

All of the above being considered the one thing I did know without a doubt is that God had said it is now time to write a book. I had no choice except to be obedient to the leading of the Holy Spirit and to write about those 13 women now! Thank you, God!

Each chapter is written in two parts. The first part of each chapter, What the Bible says about...is a concise overview of the character and challenges of a biblical woman in her setting. In the second part of each chapter, under the subtopic, Helping A Sister Out, I will share the implications of that woman's life for today's woman using contemporary women and their life experiences.

It is my hope that as you read through the pages of this book, you will find therein something to aid your healing, deliverance, restoration and/or resurrection. Each of the women in this book was healed, delivered, restored or resurrected. The one exception is Athaliah. She is an example of what can happen to you if you fail to heed God's road signs. Your soul can be lost as well as your very life. It is God's desire that not one would be lost. So read these pages with hope in your heart. This book is my feeble attempt to glorify God by *"Helping a Sister Out."*

Chapter One

Martha: Don't Sweat the Small Stuff
Luke 10:38-42; John 11; 12:2

What the Bible Says about Martha

Martha was the elder sister of a well-known family in Bethany. She had a brother named Lazarus and a younger sister named Mary. At the point where we enter her story, Jesus was passing through the city and Martha welcomed him into her home. She was busily carrying out her many household duties, when she noticed that her sister, Mary was not helping her. Mary was sitting with the disciples of Jesus and her brother Lazarus. She had positioned herself at Jesus' feet. Taking the position of a would-be disciple,[3] there she sat hanging on every word that fell from Jesus' lips. Realizing that she was doing all the work by herself, Martha asked Jesus a very poignant question: "Do you not care that my sister has left me to do all the work by myself?"[4] Before Jesus could respond, she went on to say, "Tell her then to help me."[5] She made an assumption that Jesus would take her side in the situation.

But Jesus rebuked her with delicate ambiguity for her choice of values. "Martha, Martha, you are worried and distracted by many things; there is need of only one thing. Mary has chosen the better part which will not be taken away from her." Jesus did not lay out before Martha the nature or circumstances of her distress. We do know that he did have the ability to look into our hearts and minds and touch us at our point of need. The text does not say if Martha walked through the door that Jesus had opened and laid all of her burdens at Jesus' feet. What we do know is Jesus said in no uncertain terms, "Martha, don't sweat the small stuff." Then he went on to applaud Mary's willingness to put on hold all of her household duties and learn at his feet. In doing so, Jesus accepted a woman as a disciple and Mary's discipleship can never be taken from her.

During her lifetime Martha chose the more usual woman's role.[6] She had opted for being a gracious hostess, showering her guests with hospitality. Hospitality is listed among the spiritual gifts.[7] It is the supernatural ability God gives to certain believers to extend extraordinary warmth and generosity to strangers and/or guests.[8]

Laced throughout the Bible are many examples of women in the role of homemaker. In this way, the Bible shares with us, it is perfectly acceptable to be a homemaker. Domestic Engineering is an art. Not every woman is a good housekeeper. Nonetheless, no matter what profession you choose in life, do not forget about your soul. The spiritual life of the believer should hold the most important place in your life.

When Martha became upset with her sister, Mary's preference for listening to Jesus teaching, she crossed a very delicate line. Although housework is important, Jesus is more impressed by our fellowship with him when a teaching moment is taking place. Martha's timing was all wrong. A simple meal would have been enough to fulfill her obligation to her guest. She could have given them whatever she had on hand that required very little preparation. Or she could have waited until the fellowshipping and time of sharing was over, then asked her sister and brother to assist her in serving their guest.

Jesus helped Martha and women like her realize that none of her household duties were important enough to cause her such excessive care and frustration. Martha had other things on her mind that she may have been carrying for sometime. There is a time and place for everything. When you allow your personal problems to weigh you down while the word is going forth, you may miss the blessing that the Lord has in store for you and you may also miss the answer to your problem.

Although on this occasion Jesus chose to rebuke Martha, he loved her and visited her home whenever he was in the area.[9] As we fast forward through the life of Martha, we learn that Jesus' ministry and his message were also important to her. She believed that he was the Messiah and she knew that he had great power.[10] Jesus was the one she turned to when her brother, Lazarus had his first brush with death. As time passed, Martha also grew to accept her sister's role as a disciple of the faith and dear friend to the prophet.[11]

MARTHA: Helping a Sister Out

Whether biological sisters or sisters in the spirit, all women are unique and different. At a given point in time, they may be marching to the same drum beat but their rhythm and step are not always the same. Our contemporary Martha, a woman from one of my counseling groups, yelled at her younger sister, "One day your turn will come. I'll get married and leave home, then you will be stuck with all the cleaning, cooking, washing and ironing. You will be the one who does not have a life because you will have to stay home and care for the younger children."

Mary, her younger sister, did not respond. First of all, she did not understand what was really at the root of Martha's temper tantrums. Young Mary had learned early in life that she could not win an argument when Martha was upset like this.

So she leaned on what she did know. Mary gently replied, "Martha, I have finished my task, may I help you with yours?" Mary knew she needed to gently remind her sister that all the kids had to pitch in and help with the housework at some point in time. She had read in her mother's Bible that she should not fear people when she was doing the right thing.[12] When she thought of this scripture she would smile in the face of fear, intimidation, and danger. Sometimes this made her persecutors even more furious but that was their problem. Mary always had empathy for her older sister, Martha.

Martha's life really was difficult. She wore hand-me-down clothes. And would borrow her older sister's clothes without asking. Sometimes at school, one of Martha's older sisters would force her into the girl's restroom and make her pull off the borrowed article of clothing. It got to a point that Martha would carry her own blouse or shoes to school and place them in her locker to avoid having to spend the balance of the day at school wearing something that she managed to find in the unclaimed clothes from the girl's gym.

Martha married the first boy who showed her affection. Marriage was her way out. In the beginning she did not mind being a maid in her own home. That became her profession, as well. After all, cooking, cleaning, and scrubbing floors, making the home look beautiful was all she had been trained to do. It was also one of her gifts. Her home looked like a picture from a *Home and Garden* magazine.

After giving birth to her fourth child, Martha began to notice that her husband had wandering eyes. She thought – two can play this game. Martha tried running around with other men to exact her revenge. The men bought her nice things and showed her a good time. But the fear of getting caught and the guilt of committing adultery soon slowed her down.

This vibrant young woman had been converted as a child and began attending a new church with an older relative. In church, she discovered some of her many other gifts. She began to teach Sunday school and to speak on special days. She became a counselor to women in her community. Martha became an everyday evangelist and helper to women in distress. She became involved in many community activities.

Martha had always hated her work as a domestic engineer. So she returned to school and became a nurse. Her nursing career was exciting, rewarding, and challenging. Now she was making good money. She could use it to decorate her home, purchase a car of her own, and buy new clothes for herself and her children.

As time went on she realized that her marriage was over. Her husband was spending more time with his white mistress than his own family. Martha divorced him. After the divorce, she began dating, but never found that blissful happiness that she had always desired.

What was keeping Martha pinned to the mat? She was carrying around too much baggage from her past. She was being robbed of happiness by all her past problems which she had long ago locked away in her heart. Martha had never learned to forgive and to forget. She was envious of other persons in her family who had been through the same struggles, because they *appeared* to have overcome the difficulties of life. Inadvertently, Martha passed her negative attitude toward other family members on to her children. They began to model their mother's irrational behavior. Her children never married and most of them were still living at home with their mother. In that close environment, they began to feed on each other's insecurities and irrational behavior. Small things in their lives were blown out of proportion.

Sweating the small stuff in life is getting your brain in a knot over things you can not control nor change. When your brain is in a knot, your blood can not feed your brain cells. You begin acting out based upon limited knowledge and a distorted view of reality. What you hear about a situation or see during a certain point in time is never the totality of any event. You can not control people nor change people. You can not live their life experiences. Although two people grow up in the same environment, their life's journey will be in some ways different. They are going to do what they are going to do whether you like it or not.

After listening to Martha's story, other women in our counseling session (helping group) began to open up and share situations from their lives that they felt may help Martha and other women in our group. One woman shared that she chose to put her adult children out of her home. Even their small problems were draining the life from her emotionally. She said the best thing that she could do for them was to help them financially, from time to time. Now that her children were gone, she could lock her doors at night and not worry about who she would wake up and find in her home.

Another woman shared that she really hated her job. So she took early retirement. She has just enough income to keep a roof over her head and meet her day-to-day expenses. Before leaving her job, she felt that without that job she would not be able to enjoy life. Over time she has learned to live on less income. In order to keep a certain amount in her savings account, she does take on extra work when a major financial obligation arises. But she no longer sweats the small stuff.

I said earlier that Martha had not learned to forgive. You can not alter your past. Parents are not perfect. When our parents were young, they lived their lives the best way they knew how. Some parents were even victims of their own dysfunctional past. However, after becoming an adult and realizing that things in our life are not the way that we want them to be, it becomes our time to take responsibility for our future. At that point, we have a choice. We can get away from the situation and/or get some help. Professional help is a must if the problem has gone on for years or if you feel that it is too complicated for you to handle on your own. However, I would like to share some things you may wish to try first.

Focus your energy on learning to forgive persons who have caused you pain. "Forgiveness is the act of rendering null and void the penalty owed, by a wrong to an offended party."[13] Be realistic. What happened to cause you pain? Do you remember the details of the incident? Is it the original incident that is holding you in a head-lock or is it the fact that the other person never apologized? During your lifetime, who have you hurt? At some point in our life, most of us have hurt someone. Remember words once spoken can never be reclaimed. Pray over the situation and move on.

If it is possible, go to the park or some other place where you feel at peace. I choose public open air places because the words that you exchange can take wings in the open air and float away with the wind. Invite the perpetrator to join you there. An essential step in the process of forgiveness is that the offender realizes that they have offended you. If the other party apologizes, accept their apology and move on. As the offended party, you should grant unconditional forgiveness. If you are expecting them to make amends this may or may not happen. Don't hold your breath hoping they have changed. Exhale, let it go.

There are some times a person knows they have done you wrong, but they don't know how to rectify the situation or they sincerely believe that you have forgotten about it. They simply do not want to stir up old mess. It can cause a stink. One day the Lord laid it upon my heart to call up everyone that had dropped out of my life unexpectedly and to apologize to them. Some I did recall having had a disagreement with, while others I had no clue as to why we were no longer friends. God had placed them in my spirit and I was at a point in my growth that I needed to listen to God. I trusted God enough to know that there was some pain there and it needed to be relieved. I spent hours praying and reflecting before making the first call. Then I called them one and all. To my surprise every person was at home or in their office. Oh, the joy that flooded my soul as I sincerely spoke to each person. Thank you God, just the memory of those calls gives me great peace and sets my heart aflame with immense joy.

The best way to forgive is to admit that you are hurting and you do not wish to be in pain any longer. Say to yourself, I am going to go on with my life and mean it. Remember Ephesians 4:31-32 admonishes us to "put away from you all bitterness and wrath and anger and wrangling and slander, together with all malice, and be kind to one another, tenderhearted, forgiving one another, as God in Christ has forgiven you."

Martha also struggled with envy. Envy is a monster that belongs in a cage. It is one of the more difficult sins that we are willing to admit has taken up residence in our heart. Envy can be defined as "dissatisfaction at some good or quality belonging to another which is experienced as devaluing one's self-worth."[14] It is a normal thing to sure up your identity by comparing yourself with another. When a

20

person's spiritual or material possessions are perceived as challenging your personal adequacy and you feel a loss of self-esteem, you are being envious.

First realize that your heart is not the kind of cage that can hold on to envy. It will destroy you from the inside out. Envy has to be handed over to God so that it can be tamed. You are to accept who you are in Christ and build upon your own personal strengths in life. Remember what God has for you is for you. Seek your own purpose and meaning in life. James 3:16-18 can help us here, "For where there is envy and selfish ambition, there will also be disorder and wickedness of every kind. But the wisdom from above is first pure, then peaceable, gentle, willing to yield, full of mercy and good fruits, without a trace of partiality or hypocrisy. And a harvest of righteousness is shown in peace for those who make peace." Accept your own gifts, after all they were given to you by the One who has the power to grant you peace.

Go on with your life. Realize that it may never be perfect. But it is yours and you are in control of your own destiny. When you wake up each morning you are the only person who can decide how you will respond to the challenges of *your* day. Not sweating the small stuff is not only an option, it is a choice. One counselee shared that when you choose to listen to the bad news, help when you can and leave the negative stuff with negative people.

Lastly, Sister Martha was void of companionship. One of my counselees shared that she chose to have a male companion. Although two can live cheaper than one, she chose to live alone, and granted him the same privilege. She had her home and she encouraged him to keep up his own house. That way the hours that they spend together are full of sharing and excitement. Most women need a husband or a male companion. But statistics confirm that not every woman will have a male companion for the duration of her life. Some of us must learn to enjoy singlehood.[15] In any event, before you can be confident in a relationship with another person you must first be comfortable with who you are.

At a subsequent session, another woman shared that she chose to find out what really made her happy before looking for a male companion. She took the time to discover what made her laugh. She tried different things to determine what put her on a natural high. Leave off the valium and other stimulants, if you can – marijuana and other drugs are a no, no. Gin will make you sin, but a little wine is good for the heart. Seriously, she was talking about activities and forms of entertainment. She took the time to discover her personal passion in life. She made a list of her priorities, dreams and goals. Remember these will change with the seasons of your life.

Finding your center of happiness will not happen overnight. For most of us it may take months or years of trying new things and spending time with new people. Face it girls, most women need a sister-girl to share secrets with and a brother-man to be their companion and to hold them when the hormones are just at the right level. We were not created to be alone all the time.

A few good places to begin looking for a friend is at church, the grocery store, the library or the gym. Simply observe people around you in settings where you feel comfortable. I was in the dry cleaners one day and noticed he and I liked similar color tones. I met one of my husbands at a PTA meeting and another at a church conference. It suffices to say, the one I met at the church conference was the man that I had been waiting all my life to find. He was *not perfect*, I am *not perfect*. But, together we were like peaches and "real" cream.

Get to know them in a place where you feel at ease, then invite them to join you in doing something you enjoy. The second time you go out together, allow the other person to pick the place. If it works you have discovered a new friend. If it doesn't work out, move on to the next adventure. Nothing ventured, nothing gained. After all life is a glorious adventure, custom designed for your participation and enjoyment. One last word, avoid married men. The rendezvous may be exciting for the moment, but it is a sin. You will pay a tremendous price for a little dessert.

A Meditation

Martha was troubled over many things. All the commentaries agree on this point. So she reacted inappropriately. It is how we handle ourselves in the midst of troubles that make us who we are. True happiness is elusive to those persons who choose to hold on to the negative side of their life. There are always some negative reactions we can choose or some positive responses. It is a good thing to be righteous in our responses to the difficulties of life. It is a good thing to know that whatever we have been through God has all seeing eyes and he has taken in the full view of our life's situation.

Psalm 68:3 says, "But let the righteous be joyful; let them exult before God; let them be jubilant with joy. Sing to God, sing praises to his name; lift up a song to him who rides upon the clouds – his name is the Lord – be exultant for him. Father of orphans and protector of widows...God gives the desolate a home to live in; he leads out the prisoners to prosperity, but the rebellious live in a parched land."

If you choose to be negative, you will remain in a desolate state. If you choose to try to live a righteous life, not relying on worldly wisdom alone, your happiness is in sight. God will manifest himself in the midst of your situation because he is a helper to the helpless.

Pray to God, today. Lift up before the Lord all your cares. Strip your soul bare before God. Lay down all your concerns at the feet of the Lord. Then go into your secret closet, go into the depths of your heart. Shut the door behind you. Ask God to help you find the real you, the person who has been struggling and crying all these years to come out and be at peace. Listen to God and do just what God says. When you return, you will be refreshed and prepared to move on with your life. You will have gained the strength you need to face the future.

I encourage you this day to trust God to lead you through each day of your life. Then you will never be alone again. When you make an effort to reconcile a broken relationship and carry all your cares before God and leave them there, your conscience will be clear, your mind can be at peace, and your heart can rejoice. Enjoy your journey.

Chapter Two

Mary: Passionate About His Presence
John 11; 12:1-8

What the Bible Says about Mary

In Luke's gospel, Mary was passionate[16] about Jesus' presence. As her story opens we find her leading a contemplative life. Mary sat at Jesus' feet and listened to what he was saying. For her devotion to the Living Gospel, Jesus said of her, "Mary has chosen the better part, which will not be taken away from her." Jesus approved Mary's preference for listening to his teaching, thereby accepting a woman as a disciple of the faith.[17]

As we fast forward through Mary's life, John's gospel records that at the time of her brother's illness, she and her sister sent a message to Jesus. Lazarus was at the point of death and they knew that Jesus had the power to save him. After all, Jesus loved that family as if they were his own siblings. Because Jesus was on a greater mission, he allowed Brother Lazarus to die and be buried before he appeared at the cemetery. Up to this point, Martha had been the one communicating with Jesus. Martha was always the busy one and Mary was at home, mourning. This is the second time that we see Martha active, while Mary is contemplative.[18]

After being told that Jesus wanted to see her, Mary ran to him and began to confront him for his delay in coming to minister to her brother. She felt that if Jesus had been there Lazarus would still be alive. So after the accusations and the tears had been shed by all, Jesus raised Lazarus from the dead. This act caused a shift in Mary's relationship with Jesus. She witnessed the power of his presence first hand. [19]

The next time the sisters saw Jesus it was a few days before the Passover. As Jesus was sharing with them, Mary interrupted the evening's discussions and caused a scene. She took a pound of costly perfume made of pure nard, anointed Jesus' feet, and wiped them with her hair. Judas Iscariot protested but Jesus defended her. Jesus prophesied that she had bought it not to resell and give to the poor but, "to keep for the day of his burial." Jesus foreseeing his death reminds all present that the anointing is the last rite in preparation for burial. Mary has moved from being a contemplative worshipper to being passionate in service.[20]

Mary followed her heart and the unction of the Holy Spirit. We already know that she had a passion for Jesus' presence. Passionate people give their all in service. Mary did not dab a little oil on his forehead. "A little dab will do you" was not her motto. She anointed his body with the oil from the crown of his head to the sole of his feet.

Passionate people give their best in excess. She gave up what amounted to a year's wages while being passionate in her service to the Lord. When Judas became upset, Mary simply overlooked him. Judas was a taker and Mary was a giver. Passionate people are givers.

And passionate people do not care what others think when they are operating under the unction of the Holy Spirit. Mary did not take a vote to see if everyone was in agreement with her using the expensive perfume for the purpose of anointing Jesus. I can imagine that the entire house was filled with the fragrance of that costly perfume. Passionate people leave a great aroma behind. This scene between Mary and Jesus changed the entire atmosphere in that room. We know that it did because we have not stopped talking about it even unto this day. Mary's passion for his presence made a mark on the chronicles of biblical history that can not be erased.

The Bible does not give us scene-by-scene details of what happened to Mary after this point. But given Mary's passion for His Presence, I can image she was one of the unnamed women[21] at the foot of the cross on the day of Jesus' execution and in the Upper Room when the Holy Spirit took control.[22] In any event, we can be assured that the foundation had been laid and she was well on her way to living out her destiny and passion as a disciple of the faith.

Mary: Helping a Sister Out

Mary's story is one of watching the Holy Spirit manifest himself within the life of a disciple of the faith. The Holy Spirit or Spirit is the motivating force that has cue-producing properties that organize and guide spiritual cognition and action. It is this Spirit that gives rise to our passion. 1 Thessalonians 5:19 says, "Do not quench the Spirit." This text is packed with wisdom. For you see the Spirit can be manifested through us in many ways. The three ways that we are most familiar with are in prayer, praise and service.

There will be times in the life of a Christian when the Holy Spirit will place a burden on your heart to pray for a person. Sometimes when you receive these burdens, you are unaware of what they are. All one knows is that you feel a certain heaviness about a particular matter or person. If you fail to pray, you may feel a sense of distress within as if you have left something undone. The longer you hold it in or fail to follow up on the promptings of the Spirit; you will become even more weighed down.

You are quenching the sensation which the Holy Spirit gives to move us to pray. The more you do this the fewer sensations will come upon you. Finally the Spirit of prayer or the unction of the Spirit will become so dulled that it will be difficult for you to regain that feeling. You may become unable to pray the prayer that the Holy Spirit had placed upon your heart.

I heard a mother once say, "I used to get these feelings that I needed to go and see Sister or Brother so-in-so. And I didn't. You know I forgot about Sister or Brother so-in-so. Then I heard she had fallen on hard times or I heard he died." The unction to pray for others will become fewer and far between when you fail to be obedient to the dictates of the Spirit. It may even dissipate. Therefore, you are no longer a useful vessel before the altar of the Lord. The Lord can achieve nothing through you since you are no longer able to breathe out a prayer according to God's will.

A child of God should pay the cost of praying fervently for whatever the situation may be. The Spirit had placed it upon my heart to pray for a woman who was ill. At the time she and I did not have a good relationship. So I allowed the spirit of fear to give me a laundry list of reasons why I should not go to the woman's house to pray. I had done nothing wrong to this person. I knew from experience that she had problems with me. The gulf between us was her design. The longer I delayed the heavier my heart became and the more her condition weighed upon the forefront of my mind. One day the burden became so intense that I began to pray. I asked the Lord to forgive me for my disobedience. I petitioned the Lord to give me the strength to do God's will. And I prayed that the Lord would prepare her to receive me and to accept God's healing of her condition. That same morning I went to her home and she welcomed me. When I shared why I was there she accepted my prayer and my presence. As I left, I was on a spiritual high. I knew that her healing was taking place and she was already being resurrected to her new light in Christ. But I had also crossed a great divide in more ways than one; God was using me in a new way. I was also a new creation in Christ.

When you are faithful in prayer, praying as soon as the burden comes upon you, prayer would not become an unbearable weight. It would instead be light and pleasant. When you pray in full submission to the Lord, you will sense a lightening of your prayer burden because you are allowing the Holy Spirit to pray through you.

Like Mary, people who do not quench the Spirit have a passion for God's presence.[23] Today, you can also live out that passion in your praise. I can remember a time in my own spiritual journey that I would openly say, "I want to get the Holy Spirit." Although, I grew up in a home where my mother could shout while washing and ironing in the middle of the day, at that time, I felt the Spirit was a physical manifestation that only came upon you if you were God's elect and it only came upon you in a worship service. I had to mature in my faith to learn that the Spirit works from the inside out. And the Spirit will manifest its presence whenever the Lord wants to move across the altar of your being.

It is my nature to be a very conservative person, truth be told I used to be very restrained in public gatherings. But I like celebrating my birthday. I can remember at a particular birthday event, the music was playing and I got so excited. As the crowd was celebrating with me they began to chant, "Go Evaleen, it's your birthday. Go Evaleen, it's your birthday. Go Evaleen, it's your birthday." When that party spirit came alive in me, I danced all around the floor. Or as the young folks say, I got giggie.

After that I began to wonder why it was so difficult for me to get 'giggie for Jesus.'

You are to first allow God's presence to consume you from the inside before it can be manifested on the outside. Don't get me wrong. I loved the Lord and "practiced my religion everyday," nevertheless, I was too inhibited. I worried about what someone would think if I got my shout on. Not wanting to be out of order in worship, I wondered when was the appropriate time to openly give words of praise. There had been innumerable times in my life that I just wanted to run for Jesus or jump for joy. However I would hold myself, praying, crying and rocking. My husband who often observed me in worship had said that one day I was going to explode. But somehow I knew the Holy Spirit would teach me when to cease from prayer, and turn my petitions into thanksgiving, through physical praise.

Then one day at the close of the morning message after the doors of the church were opened (the invitation to discipleship was extended) I looked up and a young man whose soul I had been praying for was at the altar renewing his confession of faith. I recall thinking, "Lord, I wish I could shout for joy." I could feel my own heart beating wildly. Then, 'something got a hold of me' and would not let me go. The 'Spirit of the Lord' was moving from the tips of my toes to the mold of my head. When the 'Spirit' took control, I hit my head on the back of the pew. Later I was told they heard the sound of my head hitting that pew all the way in the back of the church. I did not feel the pain.

All I know is that God had answered my prayer, this young man had come to Jesus and I just had to praise the Lord. I didn't care that the congregation was trying to listen to the young man's statement. I didn't hear the deacons vote him in. I did not care that my new suit was wringing wet with sweat. I did not realize my Bible had gone flying across the rostrum. All I knew was God had answered my prayer and I couldn't contain myself. I had to praise the Lord. This form of physical manifestation of the Spirit, the shout, had been within me all along. It was crying and struggling to come forth. And I had been *quenching the Spirit*.[24]

For those persons who sit up in church (knowing what the Lord has done for you) and rock away their praise, I want you to know that it is far better to get up and move. The Bible teaches us that everything that has breath should praise the Lord. David danced when the Ark of the Covenant was recovered. In fact, he shouted right out of his clothes. Remember you can not and should not try to manipulate spiritual praise. Not every person will shout all over the church. Don't compare yourself with anyone else in worship. Allow the Spirit of the Lord to take control of "you."

Usually my shout is more humble. I simply lift my hands to heaven and cry out to the Lord. That is how God moves across the altar of my soul. My mind moves so rapidly in worship that sometimes, I have already latched onto the behavioral purpose (meaning) of the sermon and I am ready to celebrate while God is still developing the sermon idea in the minds of the rest of the congregation. So God oft times has to slow my thought processes and allow me to savor the message while it is still in process. Many of us would get far more out of the worship experience if we were to follow the dictates of the Spirit and allow the Lord to take control in body, mind and spirit. A word of caution: don't wait for the worship leader or the praise team to help you to discover that the Lord is in the church house. God's spirit is your choreographer.

The Spirit has been within you all along and he is crying, he is screaming, he is struggling to be released so that you can be set free in worship. Don't be concerned about what people will think. Forget church protocol, God is not a God of disorder. *Whatever you do under the power of the Spirit of the Lord is in order with God.* If the Spirit moves you to clap your hands, clap your hands. If the Spirit moves you to stomp your feet, stomp your feet. If the Spirit moves you to run for Jesus, run for Jesus. If the Spirit moves you to cry out to Jesus, cry out to Jesus. If the spirit moves you to shout for joy, shout for joy.

And when I'm getting my praise on don't hinder me. One day, God is going to help the church to realize that shouting folks do not need to be restrained. Just stand by to assure they do not fall and injure themselves and be ready to cover a lady's bottom if her dress leaves too much in view. As long as a person has not fainted and is not in respiratory distress allow their praise to run its course. The Spirit will also tell another believer when to comfort a person with a hug or a word of reassurance.

Lastly, the Spirit may also manifest itself in a passion for service. Mary was uninhibited in her service to the Lord. She anointed His body and wiped the excess perfumed oil from his feet with her hair. Ladies, Jesus' body has already been anointed. That is why the women did not do it at the tomb. Today, our role is not to go looking for Jesus in the person of the preacher/pastor so that we can anoint his body. That type of behavior would border on religious psychopath disorder (The use of religion to justify abnormal behavior.).[25] Our role is to be obedient to the dictates of the Spirit in our service to all of God's people. (See Chapter 8 for more on passionate service.)

The problem that so many persons experience today is we are too busy asking what's in it for me and not what can I do for Him. Jesus left us with a blueprint of mission and ministry when he said "go into all the world...teaching them to obey everything that I have commanded and I will be with you."[26] From the beginning of his public ministry, Jesus left no doubt about the purpose and passion of His ministry.[27] Being passionate for His presence is the purpose for which we were created and it should be our passion to continue the journey that Jesus laid before us.[28] Our passion works its way out in our prayers, in our praise and in our service. Do not quench the Spirit. Move forward with your entire being focused on Him. When you attune your entire being to the Spirit of the Lord there is freedom.[29]

Chapter Three

Athaliah: Generational Curses
2 Kings 8:18, 27; 11:1-16;
2 Chronicles 22:2, 10-12; 23:1-15

What the Bible Says about Athaliah

If you take a precursory look at the life of Athaliah, one would say she was rotten to the bone. The Deuteronomist writer in 2 Kings 8:18 attributes the adverse moral conditions during Joram's reign to the fact that he was married to Athaliah. In a manner of speaking, she was a chip off the old block. She was the granddaughter of King Omri and the offspring of King Ahab and Queen Jezebel. Her husband's reign was wicked. He killed off all possible rivals to his throne silencing forever any opposition to the pro-Israelite policies of the king and queen. He eventually died of an incurable disease leaving his son, Ahaziah, to ascend to the throne. His reign was so wicked that he was not buried in the tombs of the kings because no one regretted his death.[30] This had to have some type of adverse effect on his widow, Athaliah.

Ahaziah, her son, was made king at the age of twenty-two years. He was also an evil king. This was not surprising, Athaliah was Ahaziah's counselor. This appears to have been a normal role for the queen mother in the monarchies of Israel and the ancient Near East. The queen mother held a defined position of great political power. And like mother like daughter, Athaliah was the mirror image of her own mother Jezebel in her effective wielding of that power.[31] Ahaziah lasted only a year before some unwise alliances led to his death. Enraged, Athaliah went about killing all the royal family of the house of Judah, which were primarily her own grandchildren. Only one child escaped her wrath.

Josheba, the half sister of Ahaziah, took her infant nephew, Joash, and hid him from his grandmother, Athaliah, in the temple for six years. Athaliah proclaimed herself queen and ruled for several years.[32]

When the time was right, all the heads of the families of the Levites, the house of David were called together by the priest of the Lord, Jehoiada. After being assured that young Joash was the rightful successor to the throne of David, they pledged to him their allegiances. When Athaliah learned of this, she was livid and cried out, treason. But it was too late for her to do anything to change the order of events.[33] Athaliah unwittingly had tried to destroy what God had set in order, the divine succession of the throne of the house of David.[34]

She had been effectively overthrown by what amounted to a palace revolt. Her own military troops had turned against her. Her personal body guards were useless.[35] She was taken out to the horse gate, and quickly disposed of. This coup that led to the eventual death of Athaliah was orchestrated by her own brother-in-law, Jehoiada, the temple priest.[36]

When I first read Athaliah's story I thought to myself, what woman with an ounce of decency in her would kill her own family. But even in the biblical text life is not always what it seems. Athaliah was of royal blood line. She had all her needs met and then some. But it was not enough. She grew up in a family where idolatry, corruption, indecency, greed, murder, and sexual perversion were the norm. She knew only the deviant side of life. The Jewish moralists of her day were considered fanatical and weak. Her own mother had sent the prophet, Elijah running for the hills in a state of depression. God had to intervene to save Elijah from suicide. But, Elijah's life was never the same after his encounter with Athaliah's mother.[37]

The false prophets of Athaliah's day catered to her every whim. Power was a trophy to be gained at any cost. Her lineage included a wicked grandfather, a weak-willed father, and a depraved mother whose life also came to a horrific end. Imagine growing up in her sandals, the third generation of a cursed family. The world either fears or hates your family. So they take it out on you. Rather than being shown love and taught to give love in return, you learn how to survive by getting them before they have a chance to get you. It is a crime and a shame that Athaliah was unable to recognize a positive role model to emulate among any of the people within her midst. She never found inner peace. Athaliah died long before she reached the horse gate. Athaliah's death sentence was simply carried out on her physical body that day when she was removed from the church and the presence of the remnant child that God had protected from her wrath. She had already died within her heart when she chose to kill her progeny. She died the way she had lived, tragically.

Athaliah: Helping a Sister Out

Athaliah is a prime example of what happens to persons who are unable to break free from generational curses. Generational curses as the term is used here are those wicked factors or traits that appear in more than one generation of a family. They are sins, transgressions or dysfunctional behavior. They are also adverse, destructive acts they can lead to sin and loss of communion with God. Generational curses are the cause for some of our discomfort with life. They not only affect the members of the family with the curse, but others who seek communion with them can also be affected. Some families have a predisposition to certain sins, transgressions or dysfunctions.

Athaliah's story is unfolding around us each day. We watch persons with the Athaliah syndrome on television and read about them in the newspaper. They are part of a family with a history of child abuse or incest that shows up generation after generation. I am aware of one family where the males of each generation have abused drugs and most of them have been arrested for possession and sale of illegal drugs. Half of the male members of a single generation of this family are incarcerated. The next generation is following in their footsteps.

Another family has a history of children being born out of wedlock to multiple fathers. They add to this a legacy of abusing the welfare system generation after generation. As the young women in the family come of age they begin having children in order to qualify for public assistance. While some college educated persons take advantage of the welfare system, many of the welfare abusers whom I have encountered are school dropouts and will not stay in a trade school long enough to acquire the technical skills necessary to obtain gainful employment. They enroll in a school and remain long enough for the county or state to verify that they have met certain requirements and then they disappear from school. Still others have a basic education but have decided it is either less expensive or less stressful to manipulate the system than it is to work a nine-to-five job. Some lack the social skills necessary to acquire and maintain gainful employment. As social reform laws are being written off the books, these families are becoming a part of the growing homeless population.

Some of these families are victims of their own failure to seek a better life for themselves. They have become slaves to their individual family's norms or to the norms of their extended family group, which are not in keeping with the norms and values of the greater society. Others have certain dependencies that require extensive counseling and treatment. Many have low self-esteem. And countless others do not have the social and academic skills to process all the necessary forms and be cognizant during the required interviews. They need someone to take the time to guide them through the system.

At some point in our life any number of us have had a little of the Athaliah syndrome in our own family system. At times when disciplining my children, I have remarked, I have become my mother. I would catch myself shouting the same dehumanizing words at my children that my mother shouted at me, and her mother shouted at her. I had to learn other words to use to express my displeasure and other methods to correct the behavior of my children.

A friend shared that for as long as she could remember her father had always kept a mistress. Her husband had one and her brother had recently begun having an extramarital affair. The grandfather's mistress sat with the family during his funeral and was included in his will. The family referred to this as the "curse of the Cofer men." It was accepted within the family that no one woman could meet the sexual needs of a Cofer man. So the women in the family carried their crosses, while the men did their thing. She and her sister-in-law were in attendance at a conference where I was speaking. The sister-in-law asked my advice on the situation. She said that she was very comfortable and confident of her sexual abilities and she did not wish to share her husband with another woman. She also did not want her two sons to grow up and model the behavior of the Cofer men.

My advice to the two women was to call a family conference, first among the women. They needed one another's support. The next step was to seek out a therapist who could assist them. The third step was to meet with the men involved and to lay their cards on the table. With the assistance of the therapist, the family came together to challenge and to alter the family reality.[38] They soon discovered that what they thought was fact was a lie that began with the grandfather when he wanted the best of both worlds, a wife and a mistress. He had convinced his wife that she was inadequate in the bedroom. Telling her that he did not want to divorce her and cause her shame, he kept up two houses. Following his death, the grandmother remarried and had no problems with her sexual prowess. But she had failed to disclose her husband's lies. So what had begun with her husband had continued through three generations.

If we choose to accept dysfunctional behavior in our lives, we are contributing to our own destruction. A case in point involved two women that I assisted through a non-profit faith-based social service ministry. For purposes of anonymity, I will refer to them as Athaliah and Joy.

I had been told by several persons in the community that a younger sister of a student at the center was hiring herself out to do freak-parties.[39] I refused to feed into this rumor-mill and dismissed the conversations as mere gossip. Then late one evening as I was leaving the center, a young man pointed out to me the young lady in question. She was hanging in the shadows against a car with an older man. After a brief prayer, I gathered up the courage to approach them and to greet the young woman by name. I will never forget that night. She did not appear to be surprised that I knew her name. The man excused himself and went inside the downstairs café. As she and I talked for about an hour, various men came up to her and she would simply say to them that she was busy and she would see them later. Adding the comment, "You know where to find me."

I did not condemn her for her actions. Initially, I talked about the center and the hope that I had for people within the community. She shared that the community was not a good place to live and there were a lot of people around that area that could really use my help. Then I shifted the conversation to her and her hopes and dreams. She was very open and told me her life story in miniature.

She was an "A" student but she had been having sex, drinking and taking drugs with boys at her old school. She became ill and dropped out of school two semesters prior to the time I met her. She wanted to go back to school but she was embarrassed. If she went back to her old school, she felt that she would be the object of a lot of gossip. She said most of the kids in her old school knew what she had been doing on the street. Then she began to share some of the things she had been "accused" of doing. I never asked her if any of it was true. I simply listened until she had talked out. I believe she was grateful to find someone who would listen and not condemn her. I did ask her if she could do anything with her life that she wanted to, what it would be; she said she wanted to finish school and become either a teacher or a doctor. I told her that I knew how she could make that happen. The man came back with her food and she said that she had to go. By now it was late and all the businesses around us were closing. I offered her a ride home but she said the man was a friend and he would look out for her. She assured me that she was headed straight home and that she would come to see me at my center the next day. As I stood there watching them drive off my heart began to ache. I knew that this would not be our last interaction. I made myself a promise that if she did not show up the very next day, I would go and find Athaliah and help her.

The next day when her sister, Joy, showed up for class, I called her into my office and asked about Athaliah. She told me that she really had a problem with her and that she refused to go to school. She confirmed that her sister was on drugs, smoked too much, drank, was a prostitute and did freak-parties. She said when she came down on her sister and demanded that she straighten up her life, the younger sister would run away and stay gone for days. I asked about the parents. Her parents were divorced. The father had remarried and was in one state, while the mother lived in a different state. The father did not pay child support but the sisters felt that he would purchase school clothes when asked. The mother had worked out a deal with the older sister, Joy. The mother kept one of Joy's sons in exchange for Joy keeping Athaliah. Joy had four children of her own and was expecting when we first talked.

Their mother had also abused drugs and was previously a prostitute. She would leave her younger children with Joy for days on end. I was not surprised that Joy got pregnant and dropped out of school at an early age. Their mother had carried the family from one shelter to another and they had lived in a series of foster homes. While they were together as a family, some days they literally slept on the streets. One day Joy decided that she was not going to live in another foster home. At that point she became parent and provider to her younger siblings earning money and food anyway she could. After getting in trouble in one state she moved to Atlanta to have a better life. Their mother soon followed.

One day the mother consumed some bad drugs and almost died. She went into rehab and when she was released, the mother went back home to her mother leaving young Athaliah behind. This was one of several times that this mother had abandoned her children. The girls disliked their mother for her lifestyle and for neglecting them but they were both modeling their mother's ways. They were cursed.

Joy lived with a drug pusher who abused her. He had made advances toward Athaliah so Joy allowed her to live with another woman in their apartment complex. She said that this was temporary and when she saved up enough money she, her sister and her children were going to move to the state where her mother and grandmother resided. The sad thing was Joy did not have a job and she was already three months behind on her rent. She declined my offer for bus tickets for her, Athaliah, and the children to go to the grandmother's home. Joy wanted to stay where she was until she completed her education.

She was in our General Education Development (GED) Class but she had high absenteeism. I later learned that her boyfriend did not like the idea of her coming to the center for classes. One day he showed up and said that he also wanted to earn his GED. On the days that he would come to class Joy was nowhere to be found.

Some days when Joy would come to class she would have visible bruises over her face and extremities. When workers at the center tried to convince her to seek help she refused. On one occasion, I could not take it any longer and I called her into my office and shared with her the choices that were available to her. She and her children could go to a home for battered women at an undisclosed location. There she could finish her GED program and they would help her find a job and get her own place. Or she could have her boyfriend arrested and he would be barred from her apartment. She could then continue at our school and complete her classes. In any event, she could not continue living under her present conditions because her life was in jeopardy, along with the safety of her children and sister.

That night Joy went home and told her boyfriend about our conversation. We did not see her for over a week. When she returned she came to my office with bruises over her body again. This time she told me that after he beat her, she had tried to commit suicide. We got Joy to a healthcare facility and made arrangements for a friend to keep her children. She did not want them to go into the custody of the Department of Family and Children Services (DFACS). She shared some horrible experiences that she and her children had suffered in foster care and in shelters. Her youngest son, who was only three years old at the time, had oral herpes contracted in a shelter from a woman who was his caregiver. After this she went to counseling for a while but dropped out. She never told the police where to locate the boyfriend.

Joy was a woman who people in the community said would not harm a fly but she was always getting into fights. She would take on other women and men if they disrespected her. She always ended up on the losing end of the battle. We had to withdraw her from school on two occasions for disruptive behavior. On one occasion while I was away attending a training conference, Joy called the police for another student and had the police come to the center. She and a young man in the GED class had gotten into an altercation two or three days before. He had tried to walk away and she had attacked him. While he was defending himself, she was injured. She did not call the police at the time. They saw each other several times over the weekend but she only called the police after she told her story to the entire GED class and he disputed the order of the events. They were both expelled from class for getting the center and other students involved in their personal dispute.

I was able to get the younger woman, Athaliah, in school. Her school record was spotless accept for the absenteeism. However, when we tried to transfer her to the local high school the principal would not accept her. He said that her reasons for not starting school at the beginning of the school year were an indication that she needed to be in an alternative school. He dismissed the fact that she was a straight "A" student. I did not push the issue because her sister did not have legal custody of her and she had run away from DFACS custody on several occasions. The principal probably had a better understanding of what I was up against than I did at the time.

We were able to obtain the appropriate documentation from Athaliah's mother after I threatened to notify DFACS of the child's living conditions and the location of the mother. So I entered into an agreement with the mother, Joy and Athaliah. As long as the child attended school, stayed off the streets, and got medical and psychological assistance I would keep silent. This meant I had taken on the responsibility of being an advocate for Athaliah.

Our first trip to the teen clinic was a culture shock for me. While at the teen clinic in Atlanta, I was informed that in the United States, an estimated 15.3 million new cases of sexually transmitted diseases (STDs) occur each year, at least one-quarter of them among teenagers. The area where my center was located was just on the periphery of the highest rate of reported STD cases in Atlanta. There were at least sixty teens that passed through the clinic in that one evening. Some were seen, the others left after waiting for a while to see a doctor. Some young ladies were there because they had contracted a sexually transmitted disease (STD) from their boyfriends. Others were there for pregnancy test. Still others were there for follow-up treatment. The parents who accompanied a few of the boys and girls looked exasperated. My fears were confirmed, Athaliah did have multiple sexually transmitted diseases (STDs). I also had her tested for HIV/AIDS.

While at the clinic, I learned all of the misconceptions that had been fed to this child about her condition by the men and boys she had been with. On the day of our initial visit, we determined that she had never been properly treated in the past and she had been re-infected. I also learned that she was a teen mom and she had a two-year-old child in foster care. We remained in the clinic until late that night talking to a social worker and a counselor. Teens can go to the teen clinic and receive treatment without the consent of a parent. But there I was asking questions and making suggestions to Athaliah about her treatment. The staff was curious about me, and asked for a business card and my driver's license. I learned later that they had called my office while we were in the clinic using the number from the business card that I had given the receptionist. The clinic number had shown up on my caller ID. They probably ran a background check on me with the local police department.

We made several other visits to the clinic. I never asked the results of her AIDS test. I don't believe that I would have been able to handle it if it had been positive. I prayed continuously that her test would come back negative. I did learn later from her sister that Athaliah will forever have a positive on tests for certain sexually transmitted diseases. This would be her thorn in the flesh. But, at this point the AIDS test was negative. God does answer prayer. She had been sexually active with persons who were known to be positive for HIV/AIDS and had come out uninfected.

The father never sent money for school clothes and the alternative school required that students wear the school uniform or receive demerits. If you fail to earn the required number of points in alternative school you are lost. These particular schools do not offer graduation, they are a holding station. You either transfer back to a regular public school or to an alternative school that issues a general diploma that is in the same category as the GED. The other option available to these young people is to drop out of school altogether. So I used my personal funds to get her outfitted for school. I also called in favors from friends and my Board of Directors for the center. That school year we outfitted several kids from the community, who I had gotten back into school.

I also used my personal car to transport Athaliah and other children from the community and from shelters when they would oversleep in the mornings, or if I got them in a shelter that was not on the school bus line for the alternative school. My personal car became their bus. In hindsight, the better way to have handled the transportation would have been to contact Task Force for the Homeless and obtain Marta tokens. Then the parents could have spent a few hours riding the bus with their own children to school. This would have made the parents more responsible. I also learned that the public school was supposed to provide tokens for these children if they could not get a school bus rerouted to pick them up and deliver them to a safe area near where they lived. When I discussed transportation with school officials not one of them mentioned free transportation tokens. A lot of what I have learned about helping the homeless has been through trial and error.

You would think that if someone went out of their way to get a child back into school, buy her clothes and give her money for personal items, she would go to class and apply herself. No, that is not what happened with this young girl. She had the taste of freedom in her blood, she had the need for drugs in her system, she had the joy of sex on her mind and it was hard for her to go back to a child's life with rules and regulations. She stayed in school two months and she began skipping classes, then entire days. The excuses ranged from, I overslept, to I needed to keep my sister's children, to I spent the night with a lady who keeps my sister's children and I did not have bus fare to school. When the school counselor got around to checking on Athaliah, she had already made up her mind to drop out of school again.

To add fuel to the fire, her sister Joy came to my office one day and shared with me that she wanted to drop out of the GED class and go back to regular school at age twenty. She wanted to graduate, walk across the stage like her younger sister and get a real diploma. She wanted to go shopping for a prom dress and attend her senior prom. We talked about the alternatives that lay before her. She could attend evening school, earn a regular high school diploma and attain all of her dreams. I helped her to make a list of everything she needed to do to make this happen. It would also require her getting a baby sitter for four or five hours in the evening or convincing Athaliah to watch her children. This was the last time either sister attended school. I did meet with them several more times but an argument between the two sisters always ensued. When I met with them separately they each blamed the other for Athaliah not being in school.

When one person tries to break the cycle of a generational curse, the other family members may turn against them. Joy's boyfriend turned against her each time she tried to attend school on a regular basis or tried to work at a legitimate job to earn her own money. Joy turned against Athaliah when she tried to attend school or work a legitimate job. They both had turned against their mother when she tried to get her life together.

The grandmother had promised both young women on numerous occasions that she would get them their own apartment and sustain them the way she had done their mother until they were able to carry their own weight, if they would move to her city and try to make a decent life for themselves. They never took the grandmother up on her offer. The grandmother was the only one in the family who was not deceived by any of the women. She said that her role now was to pray and wait on God to intervene.

One day I simply informed Joy and Athaliah that I was going to call their mother and I did while they were in my office. The mother was in denial. After I literally threatened to call DFACS on her that very day, she promised to come to Atlanta and pick up the younger daughter. She did not come for two weeks, but she did carry the child home with her and got her in a counseling program.

Joy, on the other hand, did not fare as well. Her boyfriend was arrested on drug possession and she was evicted from her apartment. The last time I saw Joy she told me that she was really ready to get her life together this time. She was not doing it because someone else told her she needed to change her ways. She stated that she had been praying and this time she was going to do it all right. She was also attending church with one of the employees at the center. Joy said that she was enrolled in a cosmetology class in a woman's basement and she wanted to know if she could get her GED pre-test scores from the center to transfer to the

Public School Adult Learning Program. I told her that she could and we would help her in anyway possible.

She also said that she wanted me to know why she had called the police to come to the center while I was out of town. I told her it was not important now. But she said that she wanted me to know that she was not a bad person and that other people are always taking advantage of her. I listened and we had prayer. Somehow, during the prayer I knew that I would not see her again. I cried and she cried and we parted company that day. During the middle of the night, I received a call that she had been killed by a bullet to the back of her head. Her suspected killer was a fifteen-year-old boy trying to make a name for himself by robbing Joy and another man of their drugs and then murdering them.

When the family came to Atlanta to claim Joy's body and to pick up her children they called to thank me for all that I had done to help the two sisters. Athaliah said that she would never forget my kindness because she knew for certain that she would have been in the hotel room with her sister. She felt that she would have been killed along with her sister if I had not taken the time to call her mother and insisted that she leave town with her. She was now praising God that we had forced her to go home with her mother. Athaliah continues to call me from time to time and she is almost finished with her evening classes. She is trying to test out of school early and go on to a junior college. Her mother confirms that she is staying in counseling for drug dependency and other problems. She has been clean for almost a year now.

Athaliah states that she takes her life one day at a time, weighing the affects of each of her choices. She has given up drugs and prostitution. She is working hard to quit smoking cigarettes. She only drinks on the weekend, never on a school night. Athaliah is systematically dropping one vice at a time. She works a part-time job to help support herself. She is reading her Bible and trusting God for direction. One of her greatest joys now is attending church. She went on to say that she knows God has forgiven her for her many sins and God will see her through until the end. She thanked me for my prayers and all the prayers of the people who had her best interest at heart. I asked her to stay in touch and to let me know when she graduates. If it is God's will, I will attend her graduation.

Then I shared this scripture with her, "On him we have set our hope that he will continue to deliver us, as you help us by your prayers. Then many will give thanks on our behalf for the gracious favor granted us in answer to the prayers of many." I told her that Paul would not have prayed so fervently and asked for the prayers of others if he had felt it would not have made a difference in his own life and the lives of those whom he was called to work with in the ministry and those whom he was called to serve. I confessed that I had shared her story keeping her name confidential. Many people were praying for her success in life and that as God grants victories to her day by day, we all share in her rejoicing. She was pleased to learn that so many people were praying for her. Then she mused, "So that's why those ladies bought me clothes and stuff. Thank them again for me."

Each time my thoughts turn to Athaliah, I am reminded that she was rescued not by my efforts alone but by the prayers of persons that I had shared her story with and the prayers of her mother and grandmother. She was also rescued by all the teachers and counselors who had intervened on her behalf. What made the difference in Athaliah's life? I believe it was a combination of things. Her being able to break the generational curse could be attributed to the prayers of a devout grandmother, a recovering mother turned positive role model, a center staff and Board of Directors and a struggling minister. It also helped to have teachers and counselors who stood their ground and would not allow her to manipulate them nor the system. But most of all it was the determination of a young girl to rise above her circumstances and claim life over death.

Breaking generational curses is not easy. But the first step is realizing that your behavior is destructive. The next step is to commit to change your own behavior. Get professional help, don't delude yourself. The person who is able to overcome chronic conditions and addictions on their own is the exception, not the rule. You must also realize that not all of your family and friends will be happy about your decision to step outside of the group. You may have to go it alone. But we are never really alone. There is a source of support that is out of this world. There is a power up above who is waiting for you to ask for help. Psalm 51:1-17 helps us here, although the psalmist prayer is for deliverance from illness the main theme is for restoration to moral health. The psalmist has acted absolutely contrary to what God desires and to what God has been teaching him; but this desire of God and this teaching of God are his hope for a better life.

My three-year-old grandchild's favorite picture in my home is a wall hanging I acquired during the Eighth Assembly of the World Council of Churches in Zimbabwe, Southern Africa. It is a picture of a Chinese artist's rendition of Jesus standing at the door and knocking. I have removed it from the wall and it now hangs on a door knob at her eye level. When she visits me, she locates this piece of art. At times, I can hear her talking to the Jesus in that wall hanging, telling him about herself and asking him for things that she wants before she approaches me. I have yet to deny a request that she first made to Jesus. We can all take a lesson from her.

We are to ask God for forgiveness and for help. Seek the Lord's direction for your life. The wisdom writer reminds us that we can devise many plans, but it is the purpose of the Lord that will take root and prosper.[40] Then step through the open door. Helen Keller is credited with saying, "When one door of happiness closes, another opens; but often we look so long at the closed door that we do not see the one which has opened for us."[41] Give your problems over to the Lord and allow God to lead you each step of the way.[42] God is a burden bearer; the Lord does not promise that our burdens will always disappear. Some of Athaliah's mistakes she will live with the rest of her days. Sometimes all we need is to lighten our load, and then we can have inner peace.[43] Submit your will to God's will.[44] Surround yourself with positive people who have your best interest at heart.

Lastly, keep hope alive! Hope that you can overcome any situation that seeks to destroy your life. Hope that you can become the person that you choose to become, not by default but by hard work and the grace of God. Hope that each day God is walking with you in the midst of your circumstances and when you place your trust in the Lord, God will not let you fail.

As a minister of the gospel who was given a vision by God for an outreach ministry, I continuously give my all to be a sweet-smelling fragrance to those in need.[45] In my ministry, I share everything that I have from knowledge to finances, to the love and mystery of Christ. My mission is to empower persons with life-changing skills for self-sufficiency. My financial sharing has left me one annuity check away from being homeless. But I count it all joy. God always provides for my every need. During my time at the center, I shared in some awesome experiences with my clients and other staff members. Their stories and journeys will be forever etched in my heart and in my prayers. I know that God placed me at that center so that some lost souls might find their way.

In order to save the Athaliahs of this world, it will take persons who are willing to stand in the gap and who are strong enough to go into the trenches where the Athaliahs live out their lives. Not everyone is called to serve in the trenches of life where live ammunition is falling. It was my call from God to serve at that particular center for only one year. Some are called to serve in their prayer closets. If you are unable to serve in the trenches, then perhaps God has called you to be an intercessor; it too is a high calling. Satan is often referred to as a 'strongman.' But we all know that a strongman can be brought to his knees by the prayers of a righteous person. The effectual fervent prayer of a righteous person gets God's attention. If satan has a stronghold on someone you know, don't just stand there - pray something. Whether it is hand-to-hand combat or talking to God from your knees in your holy language. Claim your position and give God your best in service.

Chapter Four

Deborah:
A Role Model for Women in the Ministry
Judges 4; 5

What the Bible Says about Deborah

Deborah was the wife of Lippidoth. In spite of all her family and civic duties, she found time to be in full-time ministry. She was a servant who listened for the important and graciously did the will of God.

The fifth in a line of judges, her story in Chapters 4 and 5 of the book of Judges gives us a stereoscopic view of the events of her time. Deborah, whose name translates as bee, is the queen mother of Old Testament theology, being the first woman in recorded biblical history to rule her people in the same capacity as her male counterparts. She possessed the ability to discern the mind of God and to relay God's thoughts to others on the Lord's behalf. As a prophetess of the Most High God, she showed humility and a willingness to serve. Therefore, God entrusted to her the spiritual and the physical lives of the tribes of Israel.

Her open-air courtroom was under The Palm of Deborah between Ramah and Bethel in the hill country of Ephraim. She judged with wisdom, fairness and justice. She settled their disputes with the skill of a trained negotiator. She was a strategic planner who sought guidance from God. Then rightfully gave all the credit and the glory to the Lord.

God chose Deborah to deliver his people from the hand of the Canaanites and named Barak as her general in battle. Up to this point Barak had been a maintenance man, fighting to protect and defend. She equipped him for a task that he would not have done otherwise, fighting for the freedom of Israel. During his debriefing, she left no doubt that God himself would be in charge of the battle.

Barak knew that the Lord was with Deborah. But he decided not to go into battle unless it was on his own terms. He wanted Deborah at his side, placing his confidence in the presence of the prophetess rather than the wisdom she was receiving from the Supreme Lord. Because of his attempt to control Deborah and God, Barak would win the battle but another would receive the glory. Deborah did not try to 'fix' the brother. She did not influence him to change his mind or make excuses for his shortcoming. She did not strip him of his manhood. Deborah agreed to Barak's conditions but she let him know that God was not pleased with his choice and would give the ultimate victory to a woman. This implies that there were male-female role issues even in a time when a woman was clearly in a position of power by God's design. Deborah, realizing that her power came from God, simply walked in her calling and allowed Barak to do the same.

When the battle ensued, the strategy was to first kill General Sisera who led King Jabin's army and eventually to go after and destroy the ruler himself. Incited by Canaanite oppression and encouraged by prophetic sanction, the Israelite armies banned together behind Deborah and Barak. During the heat of the battle, Sisera slipped away and found refuge in the tent of Jael, the wife of Huber, the Kenite king. She was the woman who killed him; therefore claiming her place among the blessed women of the Bible. At a point later, King Jabin was also killed.[46] As a result of Deborah's leadership forty years of peace reigned over Israel.

She was also an inspired writer. Following the battle, Deborah led her people in a religious victory song. It is a poetic commentary of the events. The Song of Deborah is regarded as the oldest and most obscure of the Hebrew Bible.[47] It recounted the story of Israel's backsliding that displeased the Lord and caused them to go into captivity. Her immortal song of jubilation gave the blow-by-blow account of the greatest military victory of the era of the judges. This battle was also the only time that diplomacy was used prior to entering into a war. Deborah's song reminded the people and their enemies the Israelites' glorious success in battle should be attributed to divine favor. It said that other enemies of the Lord would exercise a like fate and the friends of God would be as radiant as the rising sun.[48]

Deborah: Helping a Sister Out

The implications of Deborah's journey for those of us who have been called by God to serve God's people are enormous. Deborah is an excellent role model for clergywomen and all other women in the ministry. She was the first woman in recorded biblical history to be called by God to shepard a congregation. Being both prophetess and judge, hers was a bi-vocational ministry. When I think of her contributions to the history of humankind, my burdens get a little lighter, my spirit is no longer downcast, my head rises a little higher, and I walk more humbly with my God. I want to keep the dream alive inside of me and I know that I can never give up.

Just as Deborah in her obedience and dedication to her divine assignment signed her name in imperishable ink on the pages of history, today's clergywomen can do the same. We have that same opportunity. When God calls us out, God consumes our heart; two hearts are incessantly poured into one another, and they begin to beat as one.

Our gifts qualify us for the ministry to which we have been called. Our minds are strong and we consume God's word and Spirit with the veracity of a hungry infant who has just discovered her sucking reflex. We draw in and appropriate God's energy so that we can be and become more like the Lord. In today's society, it is up to each of us to keep our ear attuned to the voice of God as we carve out our niche in perpetual stone like Moses was required to do when he carved the permanent rendering of God's commandments. My sisters, the journey will not always be easy.

Since my present denomination is Baptist, I conducted an informal survey of African-American Baptist female pastors in the metropolitan Atlanta area. All of the women with whom I spoke were trained in Bible colleges, universities, seminaries or church-operated training programs. Most had professional backgrounds and are bi-vocational out of necessity. My research showed that many of them are widowed or divorced. Most of them either started their own church or became pastor at the death of a spouse or parent. Only two of the women were called to pastor an existing African-American Baptist church in the metropolitan Atlanta area (South Fulton and Gwinnett counties).

A small handful of assistant pastors were numbered among the paid staff of local congregations. While a larger number of ordained and licensed clergywomen serve in positions ranging from associate minister, church administrator, and Christian educator, the majority of clergy women have no official duties within the hierarchy of their congregation. Most clergywomen serve their congregations day in and day out without monetary compensation and are the last to be considered when a pastoral vacancy arises. This is a poor commentary on the African-American Baptist church which was born out of a need for freedom of worship and equality in the eyes of God. Although women have always made up the majority of worshippers in the Baptist church, they have not looked out for each other when it comes to liberation and justice in the pulpit.

So what do we do in the meantime? We continue to devote our life to our call from God, preparing ourselves for greater responsibility. We advocate for changes in the call process and the qualifications of leaders in our individual churches prior to a vacancy arising. We market ourselves for positions of leadership within the local church and denomination. And we support those clergywomen who do get the nod from God and those congregations who are obedient to God's leading. My clergy sisters and I also offer some words of wisdom for licensed and ordained women in the ministry.

ASK God for what you want.[49] Throughout the Bible we are encouraged by answered prayers. Keep in mind that God answers in God's own time and in God's own way. After Esther fasted and prayed, God gave her all that she asked for and a nation was saved from genocide.[50] God gave Moses less than what he asked for, he saw the Promised Land but never entered it.[51] God gave Paul other than what he asked for; God did not remove the thorn from his flesh. God enabled him to bear it.[52] God gave Solomon more than what he asked for, he only asked for wisdom. God gave him wisdom, honor and riches.[53] Remember, God gives according to God's own will.[54] God is the one who opens doors. So, ask God for direction. Keep the lines of communication open by maintaining your personal devotional life. Have a designated time to be consumed by God and to meditate on God's word.

LISTEN to God first and weigh the wisdom of others. God speaks to us in various and sundry ways. It is usually during the first few years of your call to the ministry that God is proving and refining you. What opportunities has God opened up for you? Which of these has caused you the greatest sense of satisfaction? What are you really good at doing? What are your skills and what are your spiritual gifts? For most career women the two can become confused because we put so much of ourselves into everything we do. Because you were a manager or administrator in corporate America does not mean that being the undershepherd of a congregation is your divine call. Sermon delivery and counseling aside, being a pastor requires, among many other things, charisma among the people and from the pulpit. Has God given you a vision for the congregation and clearly said you are their pastor?

SAVOR some of the things that God shares with you. Some things are best left unsaid. Still, other things cannot be shared with all people because there are still the naysayers who believe that God does not speak directly to the Lord's anointed in this present age. There are people even in the house of the Lord who will turn your words against you or quote you out of context. I have always been one to get excited about God's blessings and the fact that God has given me the spirit of discernment. But I did not take the time to cultivate and use wisdom with discernment, so I would share too much, too soon. My husband would caution me that some things the Lord gave me were not to be shared, I needed to wait on God to tell me what to do with the information God was revealing to me. Speaking out at the wrong time can cause much heartache and pain. Experience and training have taught me to wait and watch God work. I only speak up when God says, Go tell! At other times, I alter my path and simply keep what God has given close to the breast.

CLAIM what is yours. There are so many wonderful things going on in the church today. You cannot do them all. David loved God so much and was so grateful for all that the Lord had done for him; he was inspired to build God a house. But God told David, no. Then God went on to say that David would be blessed in other ways.[55] David wanted to be a builder at this point in his life but God had already put in place that David would be a great nation. Don't get ahead of God. Before taking on additional responsibilities in your ministry, ask of God.

KNOW your own personality type, leadership style, abilities, strengths and weaknesses. Practice identifying other personality types by observing people you interact with on a day-to-day basis. Which ones do you gel with and which ones do you have to work at getting along with? Take a course in personality types if you know that you need help in this area.

RESPECT the gifts of others and their right to be empowered for the ministry. Serving God is no one-woman show. If you shut others out, you will weary yourself and there will be no one to hold up your arms. Then the ministry will lose ground or at worst it will develop serious splinters or topple. There are some thirty or more spiritual gifts referred to in the Bible. Each of us is given grace according to the measure of Christ's gift.[56] God gave gifts to all for the building up of the church. Your role is to assist others in perfecting their gifts by allowing them opportunity to identify and utilize their gifts.[57]

PREPARE yourself for the position you want to hold in the ministry. 2 Timothy 3:15 says, "Do your best to present yourself to God as one approved by him a worker who has no need to be ashamed, rightly explaining the word of truth. This means get some type of diploma, degree or certification, field education or formal on-the-job training. Follow up with refresher courses and certifications to match the congregation's needs or your areas of interest. Sit with God and God's word until you hear God speak.

ACCEPT your differences and use them to your advantage. You are a woman; be all woman. God made us biologically different. Use what the Good Lord gave you in a manner that pleases God. Do not cloak your femininity because you are a minister. Use all of your intuition and natural instincts to serve the people of God. Preach in your own voice. Deliver the sermon from the perspective of the persons in the text using a woman's touch to aid the hearers in seeing God more fully. Women are naturally passionate. Be passionate in your preaching. A woman is usually more feeling than her male counterpart. Use this to help the hearer feel what the biblical characters may have felt during their time, contextualizing to fit this present age. Do not strain your voice. Use a microphone to your advantage.

TRANSCEND the negatives and stereotypes that are bound to pop up from time to time. If you are invited to a church that will not allow you in the pulpit, you have two choices. One, you can leave and shake the dust off your feet. Or you can preach from the floor or the basement asking God to handle the backwoods theology of that congregation. Do not get on a soap box and damn them all to hell for disrespecting you. That is not Christ-like. Preach the sermon that God gave you before you got there. Preach like that will be the last sermon that will come out of your mouth and you want to honor God with your best. I have been in the ministry for only ten years and have preached hundreds of sermons. Out of six churches where I had been asked to preach from the floor, four invited me back and into their pulpit. Of the two remaining churches, one has since allowed other women in their pulpit and the other is a hopeless cause. That pastor has said publicly that he will not allow any woman in his pulpit even after Jesus comes. The question remains will I or will I not get to fellowship with that pastor in heaven.

RID yourself of excess baggage. Each of us goes through life picking up things that we can't seem to throw away. When I purchased my third home, a nephew told me that the next time I moved he would not help me. I was moving boxes from house to house that had never been opened and some were wedding presents or other gifts that I had never used. I had china and crystal that had never been used and I would pack it and unpack with each move. But that's the light stuff. Many of us have had some hurtful things to happen to us in life, which includes the church. Our interactions with other people are influenced by our life experiences. Every now and then we each need to examine our lives and empty out before God all that stuff that we have been carrying around. There is a popular song called "Bag Lady" that talks about women who have a lot of hang ups – One line goes, "You gon miss your bus carrying all that stuff…see you coming, they take off running." The song is so true. If you have unresolved issues they can interfere with your ability to be effective in the ministry. People don't want to be around a person who has personality problems, especially if that person is a leader in the house of the Lord. So pack light and let it go – let it go.[58]

LOOK back in order to move forward. In certain cultures children are reminded of the things that took place in past generations in order to make them a better person as they grow into maturity. Profit from your own mistakes as well as the mistakes of others. If people dump on you and it's your fault, check yourself. If people dump on you because they are an antagonist, shake it off and use it as a stepping stone to rise above pettiness and petty people. There are several ways to handle antagonists, just don't get down and dirty with them. (See chapter 10.) Study biographies of famous people and put into practice what will work in your context.

REQUEST two tapes when you go out to preach. One tape is for your personal archives. You need to listen to yourself from time to time and that way you can improve on your preaching. Also, most sermons we preach in the early years of our ministry are God's way of healing and refining us. The other tape is for distribution. Most pastoral search committees want at least two of your taped sermons. If you are not looking to become a pastor but want more preaching engagements, give tapes to friends and acquaintances and watch how God will increase your invitations to share at other churches and conferences. If you are not a conference preacher or a revival preacher do not accept those types of invitations. When I was first called to the ministry, I would accept every invitation that came my way and tried to preach whatever they told me was their theme or scriptural reference. Some of those tapes are 'my most embarrassing moments.' Now, I pray over my invitations and I ask God to give me the message that is for that particular congregation.

DO cultivate your relationships with other women in the church. We need the support of other sisters, both clergy and non-clergy.[59] Accept their assistance and offer yours in return. Remember we are 'sisters on the journey.' Don't be a lone wolverine. Ask God to provide an armor bearer for you from among the women in your congregation. Being an armor bearer is a spiritual gift. Women who are trying to get their own preaching ministry off the ground do not necessarily make good armor bearers for other female preachers. Face it girls, unintentional competition can make your brown eyes green. You need a non-clergy sister to stand at your side when you are fellowshipping with the people. She not only holds your Bible and purse, but she can take notes and give out your cards. She can also be your traveling companion and driver when those tight churches fail to send an airline ticket. Remember your armor bearer is a divinely appointed helper[60] and not your maid. Although she is a volunteer, in lieu of a salary, you should cover her expenses. This can be done by requesting a double room and using your personal car. If she drives her own car, you must always purchase the gas and give her something extra. Always remember her special days. A good armor bearer is an extra set of discerning eyes. As she grows into her own ministry release her so that she too can soar.

GET to know your senior pastor and his/her spouse, if applicable. Develop a genuine camaraderie. Receive your pastor as a gift from God. The Bible admonishes us to respect persons we work with and are over us in the ministry. We are to esteem them very highly because of their work.[61] Be a faithful follower, imitating leadership, communicating, obeying and praying for God's undershepherd. When your time comes, your own pastor and that pastor's spouse can be your best allies.

DRESS like you are the person in charge. Your clothes should reflect your own personal style, body shape and personality. You should be a tribute to God from the inside out. A semi-formal outfit at the homeless shelter or a pair of bedroom slippers on your feet during morning worship does not communicate a positive message to a struggling sinner. A female preacher delivering a sermon in a pantsuit does not say 'I want to be your pastor.' It says something more in line with 'Hey, I'm one of the girls.' When a church is ready to call a pastor they will treat you like one of the girls. Do the words dowdy or sultry apply to your dress? Appropriate attire to fit the occasion is a must.

BE YOURSELF! and learn to live with some discomfort. Don't compromise on who God called you to be. The scriptures remind us to see to it that we do not become like Esau, immortal as a godless person, who sold his birthright for a single meal. Later when he desired to inherit the blessing, he was rejected even though he sought the blessing with tears.[62] Those who use cunning lies to gain a position or temporary status will pay a great price in the end.

CELEBRATE your successes and the successes of others. God has blessed you with your ministry and you are to thank the Lord for every blessing. There is a popular song that uses the phrase, *anyway you bless me I will be satisfied.* When we are serving in the area of our passion and we know that it is by the grace of God that we are performing this ministry, we have something to shout about. I am not shy about saying to folks, "God gave me a sermon or God did this or that, Oh, bless the Lord!" I share my testimony, the good, the bad, and the awesome. When we share our testimony, it can help another person who may be struggling to find their way through. One of my favorite passages of scripture is "I will bless the Lord at all times. God's praises shall continuously be upon my lips. My soul will make her boast in the Lord."[63] Celebrating your successes is a way of giving a victory report to God's people.

Many of my victories have grown out of realizing that I was stumbling and it was the grace of God that never let me fall. A friend asked the question, "How do you measure success in ministry?" I measure success not by the accolades because often times people are just being polite when they say, "I enjoyed your sermon or you did I good job." I humbly and graciously accept all compliments; they *make me smile and feel good.* I measure success by the number of souls that come to Christ and by the number of people who share that they heard God speaking to them and they are going to change their lives or dedicate more of themselves to serving God. Because of my skills, knowledge, wisdom and ministry gifts, people often ask me where I pastor or where they can come and hear me minister. I pastor or serve in ministry at *"The Church of the Open Door."* **Wherever God opens a door, I serve.** Thank you for the time it took you to read this chapter. This too is ministry!

Chapter Five

Jephthah's Daughter: In God We Trust
Judges 11

What the Bible Says about Jephthah's Daughter

The story of Jephthah and his daughter is one of the 'human sacrifice' stories of biblical history.[64] Jephthah was a brave warrior but he was also the son of a prostitute. His half-brothers, who were born to his father's legal wife, drove him out of the house because of his inferior birth. They felt that he should not participate in their father's inheritance nor claim possession of any of the family property. So, we can safely surmise that this young woman's father was a man of low self-esteem; he had issues.

Sometime later with war looming on the horizon, the elders sent word to Jephthah to come back and fight for them. During the negotiations between the elders of Gilead and Jephthah, the hook that pulled him in was their offer to make him the Prince and Judge of Israel.[65] A man who had been publicly declared the "bastard" child of his father; born to a harlot; banished from his father's house and forced to leave town; a valiant man who had begun traveling in the company of gang bangers and thieves was now being recalled to a position of authority and influence in the town for which he was homesick. He was being offered an opportunity to return to a life he so desperately wanted. They made him an offer he could not refuse.

Jephthah trusted God to bring him the victory.[66]When diplomatic negotiations broke down and war was inevitable, the Spirit of the Lord was with Jephthah. It gave him the fortitude and cunning necessary to move through enemy lines and position his army to be successful in battle.[67] The coming of the Spirit upon him should have been his confirmation that victory was imminent. However, Jephthah did not heed the road signs from God. In his mind's eye, this was to be no easy battle. The very gravity of the situation was indicated by the fact that before commencing the war, Jephthah took matters into his own hands. He made this extremely desperate vow to the Lord.

"If you will give the Ammonites into my hand, then whoever comes out of the doors of my house to meet me, when I return victorious from the Ammonites, shall be the Lord's, to be offered up by me as a burnt offering." ~ Judges 11:30-31

This vow is the centerpiece or focus of this tragic story and has been at the heart of many theological debates. Who or what in the world did he think was going to be the first to come out of his house? Or was he even thinking rationally at this point? Did he actually mean to sacrifice a human being or was it his intent to sacrifice the first animal that appeared when he entered the gate to his home? This would be unusual because an animal sacrifice was normally selected from the best of the best without spot or blemish. Nor was it the custom during this time in biblical history to drive animals out to meet the victor returning from battle. The text uses the masculine form of the pronoun, whoever; this implies a person as the sacrifice. He had no sons. Was he assuming a male servant would be the first person to come out to greet him? Human sacrifice was not a widely accepted practice in ancient Israel. Did this devout man on this occasion not weigh the consequences of his words? Or could it have been that in his eagerness to get the fighting over and to thank God for the impending victory, he could not think of any particular object to name?

I agree with the school of thought that says the Old Testament is simply too small a volume to include all customs of the Hebrews, and a full account of all the things that were done among them. There are many things that are alluded to which we do not fully understand, simply because they are not mentioned elsewhere.[68] Therefore, in my reading of this text, I choose to focus upon the significance of making vows and our resulting obligation to God. When Jephthah made his vow he placed himself under a solemn obligation and he could only be released once the sacrifice was made.

I cannot recall a more chilling and pitifully tragic story in the Old Testament than this episode in the life of Jephthah. Upon his return home from battle, his glorious victory was shattered in an instant as his daughter came dancing through the door to laud him with praise. His monumental joy was changed to utter rage and despair as he tore his clothes from his body. His feeble words to his daughter, "You have brought me very low; you have become the cause of great trouble to me. For I have opened my mouth to the Lord and cannot take back my vow,"[69] appear to be self-serving and devoid of compassion for the child. These words "brought me low" and "the cause of great trouble for me" are extremely harsh. People can say some stupid things when they are sorrowful. She did not do anything to him. She simply showed her love by celebrating his victory and God's divine favor in the life of her father.

The completion of a vow is generally associated with a state of happiness (blessedness).[70] But, in this case his daughter was quickly informed of her impending demise.

69

Therefore, the atmosphere shifted from rejoicing to lamenting. I believe she was disappointed because her life had taken a sudden tragic turn. Secondly, she was disappointed because she would never know the joy of marriage and bearing children. These things were extremely important in her society. Even in the midst of her disappointment, the young girl shows a spirit of kindness and love toward her father. She meekly requests a stay of execution in order to go away for a while with her friends and lament her virginity. This was not simply supreme submission of a daughter to her father. The vow of her father who was now the leader of Israel took on national significance. Fulfilling his vow became her duty to God and country.[71]

She spent two months on death row, in the mountains, coming to terms with her grief and sharing with her friends a period of emotional catharsis. This was a difficult time for her because she was preparing to die and was still a virgin. In Israelite custom it was a disgrace for a woman to die having never bore a child. Her very own statement confirms this. She did not want to go away to lament her untimely demise. She went away to grieve the fact that she was dying while still a virgin. At the end of her period of mourning, her sentence was carried out. In tribute to her awesome sacrifice, the women of Israel began celebrating an annual four-day fast during which they possibly portrayed a dramatization of her plight.[72] This was a small tribute for those who benefited from her family's tragedy.

Jephthah's Daughter: Helping a Sister Out

Women today are still sacrificing themselves, compromising their own value systems and denying their own rights out of love for their families. Sitting in any church congregation you will find the daughter who has placed her own life on hold to care for aging or chronically ill parents. The mother who refuses to date or to remarry because she has under age children at home. The grandmother who should be enjoying her senior years but spends her time raising a second generation of babies while her own off-spring are out doing who knows what. These women have made a choice to give up a portion of their lives so that others may have a brighter future. Most of them have made their own vow with God. Lord, if you see me through this I will forever give you the praise!

Jephthah's actions in this narrative have helped me as much as the actions of his daughter. According to the *Dictionary of Biblical Imagery*, a vow is a solemn promise made to God. It differs from an oath to the degree that an oath is an abbreviated covenant between two or more persons in which God is the witness and guarantor. The oath is represented by the act of swearing or placing oneself under a curse. A vow on the other hand always takes place in the context of prayer during times of distress. The usual formula for a vow is an "if, then" conditional phrase. The supplicant's gift is often contingent upon the granting of the petition.[73] The serious nature of all promises and conduct before God is reflected in the taking of oaths and vows. A vow is considered to be as binding as an oath and should not be entered into lightly.[74] According to Mosaic Law, the swearing of an oath in the Lord's name was a very serious endeavor[75] and the person making the vow would not be released until the sacrifice is made.

If Jephthah were here with us today, I hope that in hindsight he would say that when the Spirit of the Lord rests upon you simply accept God's favor. When things are going well accept the Lord's blessing and remain obedient. It is not necessary to raise the stakes or increase the ante. It is not necessary to try and manipulate God by saying, "God if you do this; then, I will do that."

Many of us have made vows to God. I know that I have made my share. One of my most significant vows was called to mind a few months ago. My son over the past year had acknowledged his call from God to the gospel ministry. For many years he ran from his call, until one day he came to my home and he could not sit still. The Lord had begun speaking to him in such a way that he knew it was the Lord and he had no choice but to be obedient to the leading of the Spirit. He has always been one to attend church but he was very critical of the established church. Now he could not stay away from the church. He looked for people to witness to and for persons to assist in any way that he could. On that particular day, he was doing a study of the life of Samuel. So he asked me what prayer I prayed over him when he was in my womb. I didn't have to think about it for a second.

I remember quite vividly the prayers that I have prayed over my babies while they were in my womb. With my older son, I began praying before he was conceived, Lord, if you would give me a healthy baby, I will give him back to you. With my younger son, the same prayer came forth after I found out that I was pregnant with a child I was never (medically) supposed to have. I continued to pray these same prayers until each of my children were delivered and I was able to fully examine their tiny bodies and count all their fingers and toes. Then I would rejoice over the child of love that God had allowed me to bring into the world.

When I prayed to God for the health of my babies I did not realize that I had worded my prayers in the form of a vow. I did not realize that I was making an irreversible vow with the Lord. I simply considered them earnest prayers. I did not realize that everything I did with my children would be intimately connected with God. God would be scrutinizing and assessing my every action and motive. I knew that God is intimately concerned with the way we conduct ourselves in his omnipresence. But, I had no idea that when I made my vows with God I needed to release them and I should no longer try and orchestrate their lives. After all, a mother by her very nature is a lifelong part of her children's life. So, my struggle was to stay out of God's way.

I went from making a vow for the health of my children to telling God how their lives were to be lived out. My problem has been that I would only release my sons to the Lord for short periods of time. Whenever I saw that things were not going as well as I felt they should be going, I would financially and spiritually intervene. I spent over ten years snatching them back from God. One way we try to pull people out of God's hands is through our prayers. How often have we prayed, "God, do not allow my children to suffer or struggle the way I once did!" Through our prayers we cannot make God do what the Lord does not want to do, but we can hinder the Lord from doing what God does want to do.

Sometimes in life we are permitted by God to suffer through some things in order to be purified, strengthened or to grow. Some seeds have to break open to become plants. Some buds have to burst open to become blossoms. Some blossoms have to die to become fruit. The same is true for acorns. They must fall from the tree and be pushed into the ground in order for a new life to come forth. We too have our circles of life. Sometimes there is pain, struggle and suffering in our circle of life. Many of the trials we have endured have made us the wise, strong, loving and caring persons that we are today. Because in the midst of our tribulations, God was refining us like gold.[76]

I have been a very slow learner. I have failed to heed the many signs from God that my sons were under the Lord's care and provision. At times, I failed to allow them to experience the difficulties that come to us all in life under the guise that I did not want them to go through some of what I went through in life. I chose instead to follow limited human wisdom, considering isolated incidents in their life, rather than exercising spiritual discernment. When we view a situation through a spiritual lens we take in the entire canvas. We look at the totality of a person's life; we view their situation in full and under the shadow of the Almighty God. When I view my sons' lives in this way, my soul rejoices at the things that God has done, is doing and will do in their lives. They have become 'men of valor.' I am a proud mother and I will shout it from the mountain tops. But more important than that, I will praise and thank God and 'tell my sons.'

When I really listen to the words of Jephthah's daughter, "If you have opened your mouth to the Lord, do to me according to what has gone out of your mouth." I realize that I must let them go and allow God to do with them as God pleases. I must trust God to be God. I promised to give them back to the Lord. God has already taken me up on my offer; God has a dynamic call on each of their lives. When we make our vows before the Lord the involved persons' lives are forever changed. My children are restless in this world of sin and shame. They get tripped up when they step off the path. Because there are so many challenges in this world that we all must face, they are better off in God's hands than my own.

Because I am a person of ritual acts, I made each of my sons a 'Get Over It!' card. Those cards informed them and God that my worrying days were over. My well of tears was empty and I was now ready to ask them and God for forgiveness and move on with my own divine purpose in life. I will always be there for my children, but it will be on God's terms.

Earlier today as I was taking my morning walk I traveled over the same tract of ground several times in order to get up to my targeted number of miles. On my last lap I noticed two shiny coins on the ground. One coin was minted in the year 1997. The significance of that year is that my husband died in 1997, I quit a high-paying job not knowing where my next meal was going to come from and I entered seminary. That year was the beginning of a new season in my life and I trusted God to provide and God did, abundantly. Like the widow with only a small container of oil, I was able to help my children financially. We all became debt-free.

The second coin minted in 2003 reminded me that in January 2003, God revealed to me that this would be my year for awesome experiences. God was going to do some things inside of me and through me. I am now writing a book after several years of writer's block. I have found healing in my quiet times with God. Space does not permit a recap of all of my blessings year to date; a feeble attempt at this moment would not do God justice. It will suffice to say, I am at the end of another season in my life and it's time to begin afresh.

Secondly, the inscription on the two copper coins read, "In God We Trust." Jeremiah 29:11 came to mind. The prophet reminds us that God does indeed have a plan for each of us. It is God who knows the full details of the plan. The Lord's plan is for our ultimate good. It will bless us; it will heal us; it will deliver us; it will set us free; it will cause us to prosper, giving us hope for a bright future. That inscription also reminds me I must leave my children in the hands of God, trusting the Lord to do what the Omnipotent One alone is capable of doing, and has promised to do, in the life of my family and in my own life.

Whenever you see a penny on the ground pick it up, say a prayer reaffirming your trust in God. Then keep it, those pennies do add up and from small things will come greater blessings.

Chapter Six

A Crippled Woman: Bent, But Not Broken
Luke 13:10-17

What The Bible Says About A Crippled Woman

When God heals you and sets you free there should not be a need to be healed of the same condition again and again. But when God carries us back to the same passage of scripture, the same poem, the same song, the same situation, there is something the Lord wants us to learn and we keep missing it. I mentioned elsewhere in this book that some of the early sermons that we preach are for our own spiritual growth and healing. God has carried me back to the following sermon because I failed to get the message the first time around.

Bent, But Not Broken[77]

The woman in our text had been on the church's sick and shut-in list for eighteen years. She suffered social ostracism and exclusion from the synagogue for being different. Why had she risked going to the synagogue-the church house- on this day? After all, several doctors had already given her a final prognosis; her condition was not reversible. She would be what we describe as "bent in two" for the rest of her days.

None of her friends, as an act of care or out of compassion, had encouraged her to try going to church just one more time. No, not one of them had argued that the church is a hospital where people are supposed to be healed. She had been a member of the church, served faithfully when she could. Though she hadn't been there in such a long time, she had to get there today. There was a guest preacher there, the one who had started a movement that was turning things upside down. He had earned a reputation for healing folks by casting our demons and laying on hands. His medicine was unorthodox. He would do things like spit on the ground and make poultices for people's eyes and just look at crippled people and say, "Take up your bed and walk."[78] His office hours were even strange; he worked twenty-four/seven.

So, in desperation, the woman made her way through the streets to get to the synagogue, moving slowly in her body-bowed state. Her neighbors, whom she knew only by their feet and not by their faces, avoided her at all cost. To face her would mean confronting a cripple, the deformed. She was too different. Some thought that she was demon possessed. On those occasions when they did come in contact with her, they sneered and demeaned. They could mock her and never look her in the face; after all, she was bent in two and couldn't see them.

With her body in this position, she could smell herself. The stench was at times more than she could even bear. There was no way for her to be completely bathed, unless someone else did it. Her husband had long since lost interest. After all, what man could find joy and pleasure in her emaciated body? Childbearing, which was so important in her culture, was also out of the question.

Because she was bent low toward the ground, her view of the world was different from that of most folks. The impending rain was known to her as it fell on her, not because she could see it in the clouds. The trees were known to her by the bark at the base of their trunk and by their shedding leaves that floated to the ground, not by their branches that lifted up to heaven. She was so bent over that her hair had become matted from sweeping the ground as she walked. The children called her names and ran from her. Some people thought that she was a little sick in the head. Going through life with her head tucked below her knees had surely been painful and caused some neurological problems.

In spite of all this to deal with, this broken, afflicted, tormented, scourged, lonely woman continued to inch her way to the synagogue, crying every step of the way. But she was determined to get to the synagogue-the church. So, she made her way to the church, where people are supposed to come together as a community of faith. The church-the place where people are supposed to set aside their hurts and superficial differences and reveal their hearts and revive their spirits.

When she entered the church, she was confronted by contradictions and mixed messages. People moved back so that they wouldn't be associated with her. This woman was a part of a religious tradition that taught that those with infirmities were being punished for their sins. To add to the situation, some of the leaders of the church were indignant about her coming for healing on the Sabbath. "Didn't she know it was against the law?" they murmured. Then the church members became divided into two camps-those concerned with keeping the law and those concerned about her being healed.

One of Jesus' adversaries had enough gall to get up and say, "Six days have been defined as work days. Come on one of the six if you want to be healed, but not on the seventh, not on the Sabbath." If this woman had come into our church today, I know that not one of us would have said to her, "Come back on Wednesday during Bible study, and we will pray for you at that time." Not one of us would have asked her to come back on Friday night for praise service so that we could anoint her body and lay hands on her.

Perhaps the church leaders and the naysayers acted the way they did because they had forgotten Jesus' earlier words from the Sermon on the Plain:

"Blessed are you when people hate you, and when they exclude you, revile you, and defame you on account of the Son of Man."[79]

"Count yourself blessed every time someone cuts you down or throws you out, every time someone smears or blackens your name to discredit me. What it means is that the truth is too close for comfort and that person is uncomfortable. You can be glad when that happens-skip like a lamb, if you like!-for even though they don't like it, I do...and all heaven applauds."[80]

Was this member of the human family out of place in such a sacred place? In our church houses, we welcome the straight, the gay, the old, the young, the poor, the rich, and those sliding somewhere in between. We welcome the single, the married, the divorced, and those who are somewhere in between. We welcome the famous and those trying to gain fame, the illiterate and the super-educated, the saved and those looking for spiritual resolution. As people of God, we know that everyone who comes through the doors of the church come for different reasons and they also come for some of the same reasons. They come for a better understanding of themselves and their futures. They come because the church is supposed to be a sanctuary and they need healing. That's why this woman went to the church.

The text tells us that when the woman came in the door, Jesus stopped in the middle of his sermon. This fragile creature caught his eye. Jesus called out to her, "Daughter of Abraham." This meant that she was valued; she was special in God's sight. Jesus called her to come to the front of the church. This woman was so crippled; she couldn't lift her head high enough to see Jesus. But then he spoke again, "Woman, you are free." Then, he laid his hands on her, and immediately she stretched forward, straightening her back ever so slowly. When her face met Jesus' face, the sunshine of his eyes warmed her soul, and all of her disease disappeared. His touch had penetrated her fused spine. This Sabbath-day healing was a day of deliverance from all that dehumanized her.

What gave this woman enough faith to go back to the church one more time? How was she able to experience all of the physical torture and all of the feelings that went with it without letting it kill her spirit? I believe that she was able to do these things because she did not identify herself with her deformity or her pain. She was able to experience pain, to let it move through her, without letting it possess her. She was able to accept her situation without being determined by it. She had an inner freedom that was not encumbered by her outer situation.

This woman's suffering challenged the traditions, faith, and compassion of all who came in contact with her. As we face the challenges of chronic or terminal illness or any other challenge, this woman's courage is an example for us. Her encounter with Jesus reminds us that God is sovereign. When the Lord decides to heal withered hands, restore sight to blind eyes, cure demented minds, or bring persons back after cardiac arrest, God can do it. This woman who had suffered for eighteen long years turned her problems over to Jesus, and he healed her.

And what does she do after she is healed by Jesus? Do you think she ran out and threw a party to celebrate her healing? Do you think she turned and confronted those persons who had hurled insults at her? Does she start making a list of the things that she has wanted to do for eighteen years? She may have done some of these things, but first she became an evangelist, sharing the good news of what Jesus has done for her.

In my sanctified imagination I can hear her giving thanks and saying, "Through Jesus, life's disappointments have become new opportunities. That's why I praise him! Jesus has healed my spine and regulated my mind. That's why I praise him! My depression has evaporated like the dew under the morning sun. That's why I praise him! My despair has turned to hope because of his grace and mercy. That's why I praise him! He included me when everyone else counted me out. That's why I praise him!"

Church, I believe if the woman were here and we asked her to sum up her testimony, she would say with William Gaither: "I was shackled by a heavy burden, beneath a load of guilt and shame, but then the hand of Jesus touched me, and now I am no longer the same. He touched me. Did he touch you? He touched me and made me whole."

A Crippled Woman: Helping a Sister Out

Have you ever seen a preacher shout over God speaking to her through her own sermon? That is my case every time I reflect upon the words of this sermon and the life this sister must have experienced. Today, we also have women coming to church to get their 'stuff' straightened out. Is the church ready? Is the church equipped to handle the diversity of problems affecting the women in the pews?

There are many things that naturally fall under the auspices of the church and its mission. The church has a responsibility to teach the Bible and its precepts. Telling the lost about repentance, compassion, forgiveness, correction, healing, praise and service (salvation, worship, mission, evangelism, stewardship and discipleship). It is both school and hospital.

Once the Lord has touched us and made us whole, what is our responsibility to God and God's people? Each of us has been given the same mandates by God. Jesus restated them for us in Mark 12:30-31a, "You shall love the Lord your God with all your heart and with all your soul, and with all you mind, and with all your strength...You shall love your neighbor as yourself." Then Jesus went on to say, "There is no commandment greater than these." Not only are the strangers on the street our neighbors, but every person entering our church on Sunday morning is also our neighbor. Therefore, we need to get to know them so that we can be available to assist them should a need arise.

Many of us will gladly go to a homeless shelter, nursing home or to a prison and give away tracts, serve food or conduct a Bible study, and then we leave and go on our merry way. But let some of these struggling souls come into our worship services on Sunday morning and we get like the church folks in our text. No, this is prime time. It's eleven o'clock on Sunday morning and it's our time to praise God and glorify God in worship. Don't come in here getting close to us and reminding us that we are one pay check away from being homeless. If we had not stopped running the streets or taking drugs, we too might have HIV/AIDS. When Jesus helped this woman in church on Sunday morning it should have shown us that we are never off duty in the house of the Lord. We are Jesus in their midst and our work does not stop until we steal away and take some quiet time behind our locked doors in the privacy of our own homes. So look around you. Who do you see that is bent in two? Is it you?

Before Jesus helped the woman in our text, he first stopped what he was doing and took the time to determine the nature of her problem. What we see at first glance is not always a person's real need. We are to stop doing church as usual, sitting up in church as a community of one on Sunday morning and then rushing out following the benediction becoming a community of strangers. In order to recognize when something is wrong with a person or things are not going right in their life, we must first know the persons seated in the pews. Sometimes this will mean fellowshipping with them at times other than when we 'pass the peace' during morning worship services. Fellowship is one of the reasons we come together as a church body. The other reasons include glorifying God in worship, rejuvenation, training and service.

Helping others also requires that you listen to them and look beyond the superficial. Allow God to speak to you as you become acquainted with persons in your church. I recall having sat in church Sunday after Sunday and becoming distracted by a young family with a physically challenged child. I would go over and speak to them and on the surface everything appeared to be all right. Then one Sunday, the husband said to me out of the blue, "go and speak to my wife she is having a difficult time." Before going over to her, I remembered all those Sundays that I had been distracted in church. Each time I observed her during the service, her face was not at peace and her body appeared to be tight and rigid. The Lord had been trying to show me all along that she needed someone to talk to other than her family. Her husband passed away soon after that and she was left alone to care for her children. Part of her problem was that she was trying so hard to be strong that she forgot God can manifest God's self to us more fully in the midst of our struggles. When we are weak, then God is stronger. If we would take the time to read God's road signs, we will know the persons who need our help and something about the problems they are facing.

In some cases their problems may be too big for the person of first contact to handle. That is why the entire church needs to be made aware of the resources and resource people that are available within the congregation. But remember, no one congregation can be all-things-to-all-people. Churches should develop alliances with social service agencies, non-profit organizations, government agencies and with other religious entities.

God does some of God's best work through the lives of the Saints. I often wonder what God's day would be like if we were to step up to the plate and do the work that God has gifted us to do. What service are you performing in your church and community?

Chapter Seven

The Woman with an Issue of Blood:
The Body Beautiful
Matthew 9:20-22; Mark 5:25-34; Luke 8:43-48

What the Bible Says about The Woman with an
Issue of Blood

Jesus had become a very popular prophet in the area surrounding his hometown. This woman had heard about him and when the news spread that this spiritual healer was nearby her mind must have shifted into overdrive, "How can I get to this great physician?" Her story is one of a healing story within a healing story. Someone else had gotten to Jesus first. A man named Jairus had gotten the attention of Jesus and everyone was rushing with him to heal the leader's young daughter. So she quickly devises a scheme to defy the law and touch Jesus' garment. Given her condition, she was forbidden by law to have social intercourse with anybody. She lived a lonely and isolated existence.

This woman was so desperate because she had been suffering from hemorrhages for twelve years, that's 4380 days. The severity of her problem is opened up before us in both the length of her illness and the futile attempts she had undertaken to correct her condition. Having endured much at the hands of many specialists, she was now only a shell of a woman. Her diseased body was frail, pale, weak and emaciated. Her body was in shock from the loss of so much blood. She had probably lost her betrothed, the man of her dreams. In her culture young girls were married at an early age and were expected to bare children immediately. In her condition, this was impossible because no man could touch her given her present circumstances.

She was now penniless and destitute. She had spent all of her household funds including her inheritance on ineffective physicians. They had tried one thing and then another. A hysterectomy in her culture was out of the question. She was no better now than she was when her hemorrhaging was first treated. In fact, her prognosis had grown worse. So we can empathize with this woman and the risk she was willing to take.

So she worked her way into the crowd hoping no one would notice her. The makeup applied to her dark sunken eyes, hollow cheeks and purple lips made her face look like a child's Halloween mask. It would take more than cosmetics to make her body beautiful again. So, she must have pulled her veil across her face leaving only enough room to peer out at passersby. And, all the perfume she used could not cover up the stench from her hemorrhaging body. So they pushed her downward to the back of the crowd. The rear of the crowd was the appropriate place for the crippled, the sick and rejected members of society.

She dared not approach him. A person in her condition was not only defiled, but defiled anything and anyone they touched. Resolving in her mind that if she could only touch his clothes, she would be made whole, the woman draws upon every remaining ounce of her assertive energies. She shoulders her way from the rear of the crowd to a position close to Jesus. The press of the crowd both overwhelmed her and comforted her. She stumbles and lunges forward through the maze of stronger bodies and moving feet. The woman barely touched the hem of his garment. Instantly her hemorrhaging ceases and she felt her body being rejuvenated. Both she and Jesus felt the effect of her touch. She knew; she was healed. And Jesus felt power had gone out of him.

So, Jesus turned and throws a question at a blur of faces, "Who touched my clothes?"[81] This incident is recorded in all three gospels. Luke makes Mark's touching of Jesus' clothes into a touching of Jesus moving us away from the superstitious form of the woman's faith. It is contact with Jesus that is significant. Luke completes the logic by reporting that everyone denied having touched Jesus.[82] His disciples were astonished at Jesus' question considering the crowd of people that were traveling with him.

He ignores them and continues to peruse the crowd waiting for the guilty party to step forward. Although Jesus is well aware of the woman's need, his intent is not so much to identify the woman for himself. It is two fold; he wants her to own up to her action and he wants to clarify to the crowd what has happened.[83]

Realizing she could not remain hidden, she came forth in fear and trembling. The woman bore public witness to the cause of her action and its consequences. In the presence of all the people, she told why she had touched him and how she had been immediately healed.

Only in the personal turning of the healed one to Jesus does the event reach its goal. Only then does Jesus speak of her faith. Faith is not the psychosomatic cause of healing but the subjective condition that opens you up to the miraculous working of an omnipotent God. That having been said and given the emotive nature of our story, it is better to have a superstitious type of faith that works than to be theologically sophisticated and ineffectual.

The woman's salvation transcends her physical healing and she embraces eschatological peace that is bestowed by Jesus. Her sickness does not mean death. Then Jesus goes on to say, "Take heart, daughter your faith has made you well, be healed of your disease." Jesus' remark is directed toward her prognosis not her diagnosis. Jesus not only restored her health, he restored her to society. He then dismissed her with the greatest of benedictions, "Go in peace."

Two key things happened in this story: a touch of faith by a suffering woman and a release of healing power from the Son of God. If you make one step, he'll make two. When we call upon his name, we touch his very heart. In times of suffering God feels your pain and seeks to comfort you. God's goodness turns your problems into occasions of hope. God's graciousness makes your healing sure. No matter your problem, God's mercy suits your case.

We must be careful to remind ourselves that miraculous healing is tied to God's providence and will. Sometimes, God will heal us from the estrangement caused by our uncleanness. Sometimes, we may be healed through deliverance from our sinfulness and perversion. And at other times God may release us to enjoy physical well-being. The fact that the Lord can heal goes unquestioned. That it is always his will to heal is another question. We must seek to discern the will of the Lord, that which will be to God's glory, as an authentic witness of God's presence and purpose. Our healing is given freely to us today because of the price that Jesus paid. Isaiah puts it best, "...by his stripes we are healed."[84]

The Woman with an Issue of Blood: Helping a Sister Out

An issue today is not only the spiritual, but the physical and psychological well-being of women. Today's woman is learning to separate fact from fiction and truth from superstition. We want to know what really helps our bodies. As women, we each have a responsibility to keep our bodies beautiful. Beauty begins on the inside and reflects in our outward persona.

This woman's story helps us to see Jesus' power over sickness, to be more exact his power over hemorrhaging; how our faith can place us in contact with the one who is always available to help us in times of need. It is a given to say that we are to always pray for good health, but God also admonishes us to take good care of our bodies. We are to maintain our bodies in their intended state of well-being. The human body is beautiful not only in terms of aesthetic beauty, but the intricate detail and the way that all systems intertwine. It is unique that our body tries to heal itself first without our help. Our white blood cells increase in order to fight off infections. Our blood clots to stop a wound from bleeding. Then it sends out impulses telling us what to do. If we get a fever, then we take an aspirin. When we get dehydrated, we crave water. When our immediate responses do not solve the problem, we are prompted to "get help." We seek a physician.

Our bodies are the temple of the Lord and, as such, they are to be taken care of with reverence. A proper diet is to be maintained to keep our bodies beautiful. God does not measure beauty by dress size. We come in all shapes, sizes and colors. The Lord designed us with those unique characteristics. Our beautiful bodies can be maintained by consuming the right foods in the right proportions. The Consumer Information Center of the United States Department of Agriculture publishes a brochure called *The Food Guide Pyramid*.[85] This brochure introduces us to the Pyramid which contains the six basic food groups with emphasis on five of them. They are 6-11 servings of the Bread, Cereal,

Rice and Pasta Group; 3-5 servings of the Vegetable Group; 2-4 servings of the Fruit Group; 2-3 servings of the Milk, Yogurt, and Cheese Group; 2-3 servings of the Meat, Poultry, Fish, Dry Beans, Eggs, and Nuts Group and Fats, Oils, and Sweets used sparingly. It also provides a wealth of other related information. The Pyramid is not a rigid prescription; it is an outline of what to eat each day. The Pyramid advises us to eat a variety of foods. By doing so, we get the nutrients we need and the right amount of calories to maintain or improve our weight. The Pyramid also focuses on fat because most Americans diets are too high in fat, especially saturated fat.

There are several areas where many of us go wrong. We have a tendency to eat only foods that we like based on tradition or acquired habits. We make our budget the culprit saying, we can't afford to purchase a variety of food. Some of us have fallen in traditional habits of cooking the same old foods the way Mama and Grandmama used to do it, using lots of grease, salt and sugar.

I love the story about the young woman who was preparing her first ham for her new husband and she cut some meat off both ends, and then discarded it into the trash. When her observing husband asked why she had done this, she said she did not know. She learned it from her mother. The next day, she called her mother and asked her why she cut both ends off the ham before cooking it. The mother responded because the grandmother had always done this. So the young bride did a three-way call to the grandmother. When the grandmother was asked the same question, she chuckled and said, "Why baby, I never owned a roasting pad large enough to hold the size ham required for all my children. So I cut off just enough of the ends so that the ham would fit into the pan. Then I used the ends to cook my vegetables." It is time we changed the way we prepare our meals.

We consume meals and snacks that are excessively high in saturated fats and carbohydrates and low in fiber. Still others don't like water. So we substitute soft drinks, coffee, power drinks and juice drinks. Our bodies are composed of more than 80% water. We are to drink a minimum of eight to ten glasses per day of water in order for our bodies to function at peak vitality.[86] After three months of forcing myself to drink water, I can now drink it cool, warm or hot from the trunk of my car. I never leave home without it. My doctor has confirmed that the increased water intake and decrease in coffee and food high in caffeine have been a direct contributing factor to my good health.

Women should properly care for their feet, nails, and hair. When I walk into the beauty salon or spa, I become the center of attention. They pamper me and all their clients. I place myself totally in their care for the next few hours. Each of these shops and my personal professional technicians are selected in the same way I selected my physician. My beautician and I have been together for the longest period of time. She has a quaint little shop and it is the best therapy clinic in town. If beauty shop or spa does not meet your individual standards, make a change. Find a shop where you feel good when you enter and look good when you leave.

On the other hand, it is difficult to feel beautiful on the outside when you are all sticky and sweaty. The average woman does everything she can to try and remain fresh looking and smelling good. I have suffered with heavy perspiration all of my life. So I am one of those women who has to work at staying cool as a cucumber. One of my clergy friends has ice cold hands. Since I was a child, I would break out in "hot flashes"[87] as a result of stress or a change in the outside temperature. I can remember standing up in front of a microphone at school or church nice and dry, then sitting down so wet my clothes were stuck to me and my hair had gone nappy. This was unusual for a child but no treatment was prescribed.

A few years ago, I learned that I was pre-menopausal. My menstrual cycle[88] suddenly disappeared. Menopause[89] is often a misunderstood and misused term. There is little consensus in medical and psychological literature on when it begins or ends. The degree of the definitive signs may vary from family to family and woman to woman. It is commonly agreed that women begin to "go through the change" as early as the late thirties for some of us and physical manifestations may be felt into the late sixties for others of us.

In my family women normally went through the first stages of menopause over several years before their cycle stopped completely. Their symptoms were the more exaggerated forms of irregular cycles for many years, hot flashes, hair loss, and mood swings. My menstrual cycle stopped completely for a number of months. I recall saying to myself, this isn't bad at all. I had no other symptoms of menopause. I could be as frisky as I wanted to be without the fear of getting pregnant. Then reality set in, when we sleep with a man we are also getting into bed with every sexual partner he has had. So my fantasy remained just that, a thought never acted upon.

Then one day my cycle returned with a vengeance. I began flowing so heavily, I was afraid to leave my home. I have never been comfortable with gynecologists, so after consulting one by telephone and being given the option to come in, I opted out. After months and months of continuous flow my body began to get weaker each day. Finally, I began to listen to my body and called my medical doctor. He did a complete physical, but I talked him out of a pap smear. I did not want a pelvic exam while I was menstruating. There is nothing wrong with having a pelvic examination while you are on your cycle if you are physically ill. Specialists know how to handle it.

Based on all the tests he did perform, my blood count was dangerously low. My hormone levels showed that I was pre-menopausal but my blood pressure was dangerously high. To add woe upon woe, my oxygen level was low and my respiratory test showed some obstruction of my breathing. The doctor decided to treat first things first. I was given B-12 injections and placed on a high potency vitamin. Hormone replacement therapy was not an option given the medications prescribed for high blood pressure and my chronic respiratory condition, sarcoidosis. We were able to rule out diseases such as endometriosis, enlarged fibroid tumors, and cancer.

Considering my previous medical history and family medical history, we were able to determine the cause of my medical problems was pre-menopause complicated by traumatic psychological stress and life-change stress that had resulted in spiritual depression.[90] I had recently experienced the deaths of my only brother, my father, a nephew and my husband within months of each other. The life-change stress was related to my resigning a high-paying job and walking away from a thirty-year career that afforded me financial security, power, influence, and playtime (a variety of social activities). I left that job not knowing where my next meal was going to come from; I was not old enough for early retirement. I had not yet settled my husband's estate. I entered the seminary where he was formerly a professor and found myself in classrooms struggling to keep up with students half my age. It was by the grace of God that in the midst of all that I was going through, I maintained high academic excellence and graduated summa cum laude in the top 5% of my class. The drive to excel was simply another stressor. Leaving corporate America was a positive and a negative in my life.

The plan my doctor and I agreed upon was to reduce my daily activities, and cancel all non-recreational travel engagements. My calendar was cleared of every activity except school, recreation and Sunday morning worship services. The most difficult sacrifice was the cancellation of all my preaching engagements and out-of-town travel. It cost me dearly because some of the churches on my calendar had not previously opened their pulpits to women. Although, I referred other women preachers, I was branded as a "no show." I began visiting with congregations where I would sit in the back of the church and simply enjoy the worship experience. I found this to be therapeutic and relaxing. As a result the menstrual flow decreased but did not stop for a single day.

So, I turned to the one physician that I knew could handle my case. I turned to the Lord. That is when I took my first ever forty (40) day spiritual fast. It was me, God and bottled spring water. In the middle of the fast, I began to add pure fruit juices and later added fresh fruits. The Lord and I spent hours together in prayer. I talked, God listened. God talked, I listened. And on some days there was just silence. At the end of the forty days, my bleeding stopped and has not returned.

I now have 'hot flashes' only when I am extremely stressed, ill or the room temperature takes a sudden drop or upsurge. I have learned to inquire of those around me whether the room temperature has changed or not. This helps me to determine whether I am having my own personal summer or if it's simply a room temperature variance. I have never taken hormones and my levels are normal for a person of my age. I do take natural vitamins to supplement my diet. I also modified my diet and began to take long walks in the cool of the day (early morning or late evening). I continue to drink bottled spring water with a passion. No coffee or drinks that contain caffeine ever touch my lips. I have contributed greatly to hefty dividends for many an herbal tea company. The naturally caffeine-free teas from Africa are my favorites. The one caffeine-laden weakness that was hardest for me to overcome was a daily Snickers bar or two. Now, I can be caught sneaking a Snickers bar from one of my grandchildren's candy stash or admiring them from afar as I go through a grocery store check-out line. My four-hundred-a-year Snickers habit is now a six-bar-a-year treat.

I moved forward with the dreaded task of settling my husband's estate and took the time to open over six months of bank statements. To my surprise and great joy, I found that I had money that I did not know that I had. God had touched the heart of my previous employer and some automatic deposits were just sitting there, not gaining interest. Thanks be to God! I have since given away most of my liquid assets to help homeless people but that's another chapter in my life journey.

With God's help, proper diet and life-style changes, I am enjoying my fifty-eighth year. I have none of the average problems of a pre-menopausal or post-menopausal woman of my age. My hair is healthy, my skin is radiant without makeup, and my slightly overweight body is beautiful. I am working on reducing my weight with proper diet and a consistent walking program. I have never been one to exercise. So I have to walk faster and longer. The walking is also a great stress reducer.

My advice to women of all ages is get to know your own body and do everything in your own power to keep your body beautiful from the inside out. If you are ill and can't handle your problems with basic steps to good health, please consult a specialist. Over the years, Dr. Tim, a Christian psychotherapist has become my best bud. When the rigors of the ministry or life itself begin to weigh heavy upon my spirit, I get a reality check from Dr. Tim. There are also a variety of support groups available to women. Seek the support and positive companionship of women with similar concerns. Do not sit with other women and have a pity party, the key words here are positive and support.

At the base of all of this is our relationship with God and our desire to keep the body that the Lord has entrusted to us beautiful from the inside out. When you have done all the things that you know you should do and your health begins to decline before its time, remember 'The Woman with the Issue of Blood' and seek God's divine healing. Jesus has a proven track record and comes highly recommended. The Spirit of God descended from heaven like a dove and the voice of God said, "This is my very own son with whom I am well pleased."[91] Matthew testified, "He took our infirmities and bore our diseases."[92] Even I should have been dead and sleeping in my grave, but thirty-five years ago, the Lord brought me through after the doctors said that I had a debilitating lung disease and would not live to be thirty. And that same God that raised me up off my bed of affliction just keeps on keeping me. Yes, I was once bent almost in two, but I was not broken. That's why I just can't help myself I have to praise the Lord, Thank You! Thank You! Thank You, Lord!

Chapter Eight

Tabitha (Dorcas): Your Work Will Speak for You
Acts 9:36-43

What the Bible Says about Tabitha

Hidden within the scriptures are short stories of persons who had a profound impact on the early church. One such person is Tabitha. Her story is tucked away in the Book of Acts of the Apostles. Tabitha, an Aramaic name, which in the Greek is translated as Dorcas means gazelle.[93] A gazelle is a small graceful and swift African and Asian antelope noted for their soft lustrous eyes. This description shares with us something about the character of the person. During early history names had meaning and persons lived up to the character and quality of their name.

During the time Peter was in the area of Joppa, she became ill and died. Her friends prepared her body for burial, placed it in a cool upper room and began their period of mourning. Some of the disciples in the area went to find Peter. And upon his hearing of her death, he went immediately to her bedside. They took Peter into the room where Tabitha's body was laid out. Her old friends, most of them widows, associated with her in good works or beneficiaries of her kindness, were in the room mourning.

This text is concerned with her missionary activity. Tabitha was well known for doing good and helping out others in the area where she lived. Discipleship includes following Jesus, and is also characterized by confessing him as Lord, in word and deeds. The Bible tells us that Dorcas was devoted to good works and acts of charity. Brief glances at the commentaries show that it is no simple matter to give a precise description of all of Tabitha's works. Her acts of charity may have included visiting the sick; sheltering strangers; providing for poor couples about to be married; participation in weddings, festivals, and burials; consoling those in sorrow. Almsgiving which was a major act of charity during this time period may also have been included in what she did.

The Bible does share that the weeping widows approached Peter and showed him the tunics and other clothing that Tabitha had made during her lifetime.[94] Tabitha never spoke for herself. Her spiritual gifts and skills spoke for her. Those who served in the ministry with her were her witnesses before the Lord. It is at this point through the voices of the widows that we learn something concrete about Tabitha's activities. She was a one-woman enterprise.

The widows explained in very vivid details something of what her life consisted of, as they showed Peter the beautiful garments that she had made. They were designed using fine linen and pieces of silk that she had woven with her own hands. The braiding were of gold and silver. No finer materials could be found in that Mediterranean port. What she did not make, she imported. Her garments were not only sold to the affluent, Tabitha spared no expense for those in need. There in the text part of her good works is made tangible.

Tabitha was a woman of substance. When Luke's description of her is read carefully, it becomes clear that she is valued as a philanthropist. We know that she not only worked with her hands, utilizing her gifts; she also went about doing other kind acts of charity. She took care of the widows in Joppa out of her own resources. It is no wonder that the widows wept so bitterly when she died and were the first to be shown that their benefactress had been restored to life.

Tabitha was the proper society matron, the dedicated missionary worker, doing works of charity and caring for the less fortunate. In doing her good works she utilized both her skills and her spiritual gifts. Her works of righteousness were the expression of the commitment of her whole person. She is an excellent model of what Jesus encourages each of us to epitomize in Matthew's gospel "...for I was hungry and you gave me food, I was thirsty and you gave me something to drink, I was a stranger and you welcomed me, I was naked and you gave me clothing, I was sick and you took care of me, I was in prison and you visited me." [95]

All of the aforementioned activities constitute a concept within which all acts of love and mercy are consumed. God is on the side of the oppressed and suffering. You have heard it said that God does justice for them and that God does good things for them. But the actual actions are not performed by God. The actors are not God, but human beings who are motivated by God's love and mercy. Tabitha reminds us that we are God's hands, we are God's feet. As Christian disciples, we are to utilize our gifts for God's service.

When we exercise our gifts under the power of the Holy Spirit, we do not simply give alms, like the crumbs from the rich man's table. This woman's life reminds us that we are to give out of our abundance; we are to give of our lives. As we seek to serve others, rather than moving mature men and women through soup lines like cattle through a stockade, we are to offer them a part of ourselves, our friendship, our love, our compassion, our support, and our guidance. We are to treat those persons we seek to help in ways that reinforce their self-esteem. We have been called by God to treat persons in ways that help to restore their dignity. We are to affirm others as full human beings who are no different than ourselves.

After Peter listened patiently to the words of loving testimony coming from the women, he politely dismisses them from the room.[96] Peter kneels at her bedside. Having heard the cries of the people, Peter knocks at the door of the Lord. He becomes her intercessor in the valley of the shadow of death. Then Peter rises up and calls to her, "Tabitha, Tabitha get up." Upon hearing the sound of his voice, she sits up and stares into his face.

The psalmist says, "Precious in the sight of the Lord is the death of his saints."[97] The faithful life that Tabitha lived may have been the pivotal reckoning point that caused God to reverse death; giving Tabitha a second chance to complete the work he had assigned to her hands. Tabitha, a woman, became the only 'disciple' in our version of the Bible that was resurrected from the dead. It is obvious that the death and rebirth theme is close to the heart of biblical religion, encompassing as it does a key principle of physical, emotional and spiritual life. This theme was present in Jesus' ministry. His very own life was one of rebirth, and he passed it on to each of us as baptism[98] and regeneration.[99]

Peter then takes Tabitha by the hand, helps her to her feet and presents her to the others, alive.[100] What a glorious celebration that must have been. She once was dead and now she lives. Tabitha gets to run on a little longer to see what the end is going to be. But her resurrection story is not hers alone. Death can be a tragedy, but her resurrection placed her life story on the front page of oral and written history. As the word spread about her resurrection many believed and gave their life to the Lord.[101] This page of the salvation story continues because of the life of a woman who gave God her best in service. Her name will be forever etched in the annals of history. We know that to be true because in our present time charitable missions and benevolent societies (Tabitha's Houses or Dorcas Societies) are still being named in her honor. People around the globe still are trying to live up to her statue, Tabitha a model for mission's ministry.

Tabitha: Helping a Sister Out

Time is a hyphen or dash between two eternities, the eternity you live in and the one you desire to live in. Your dash is the space between the place where you are right now and your final destination. How are you living your dash? Are you giving God your best by living up to your full potential and sharing that 'extraordinary you' with others? Extraordinary women are those of us who have taken the time to identify and develop our gifts, talents and skills. We do not place them on a shelf to gather dust. Our gifts will never rust because we oil them with gladness through selfless service.

Today, we find women in the church who are in need of resurrection from whatever is holding them back and draining their life blood from them. Vanzant in her book, *One Day My Soul Just Opened Up: 40 Days and 40 Nights to Spiritual Growth* said, "I have something valuable to give the world." God has gifted each of us with unique talents, skills, and spiritual gifts. You may not know right at this moment what it is or even value what you do. Nevertheless, as you live out your dash someone, somewhere will benefit from your presence. We saw this take place in Tabitha's mission ministry and in Jesus' ministry. Mother Teresa, Nannie Helen Burroughs, Bishop Vashti McKenzie and countless other women have sacrificed self and given their all to the cause of Christ. They were and are empowered by the Christ-spirit that lives in them. Countless other women who own their own businesses are supporting not only their families but groups of families through their entrepreneurship.

I mentioned earlier that I had given away my life savings to help others. I ran a faith-based non-profit agency awhile back. Our mission was to empower persons for economic self-sufficiency. We not only gave them bread, but we taught them how to fish. Each time I meet someone who has been the beneficiary of my benevolence, my heart leaps with joy when they tell me of their successful employment and their new life in Christ. Not one of these persons was ever aware of my tremendous sacrifice. I did not do it intentionally. It was done out of identifying a need and meeting that need. Because of the way that I gave to others, I have not gone hungry one day. I still have a nice modest home and I am able to meet all of my personal financial obligations. But even more than that, I get to see the movement of God in the life of others as they rise up and take their place as productive members of society.

An important point to remember is that your recognition may not come on this side. It may not come while you are living out your dash. Tabitha had to die before her full benevolence and devotion to Christ was brought to light for the entire world to see. Jesus had to die before he was recognized for who he really is – the child of a virgin girl, born human and yet divine, son of the living God, giver of newness of life and unlimited opportunity, sacrificial lamb. He is the savior of the world, salvation's life story.

What are some things in your life that you need to allow to die so that you can become the woman God has called you to be. Is it insecurity, fear, doubt, negative pride, low self-esteem, shame, self-aggrandizement, self-centeredness or the desire for fame? Get over it, my sisters. The preacher may never call your name and ask the entire church to stand up and applaud you. He or she may never tell you thank you. The boss may never give you all the recognition that you feel you deserve. If you are sitting around moping waiting on that, shame on you. Each day the distance of your dash is getting shorter and you don't have very long. Use your time wisely.

Paul wrote in his letter to the Christians of the Church in Philippi: "If then there is any encouragement in Christ, any consolation from love, any sharing in the Spirit, any compassion and sympathy, make my joy complete: be of the same mind, having the same love, being in full accord and of one mind. Do nothing from selfish ambition or conceit, but in humility regard others as better than yourselves. Let each of you look not to your own interest, but to the interest of others. Let the same mind be in you that was in Christ Jesus…became obedient to the point of death –even death on the cross." [102]

Remember when you are serving in the church you will be confronted by some of the same obstacles and challenges that you encounter in the secular arena. A Christian is no more than a fallen sinner, who has bumped her head, scraped her knees, broken her leg or stumped her toe and came back to church to tell about it. In her testimony, she remembers grace and mercy saying, "Get Up!" So, she keeps getting up, one day at a time, leaving the mire of life behind her and pressing forward to claim the prize of eternal life.

I tell you there is hope for those of us who remember where we have been and are grateful to God that the Lord helped us pass the test. When you step out on faith and join the faithful servants of God's Honor Roll, your journey may include a Red Sea or two. But go forward with fear and trembling, humbly depending on God for help. If you remain faithful and follow God's plan your future will be secure. Your work will speak for you. You will cross over into the Promised Land.

Chapter Nine

Rahab: The Heart of a Prostitute
Joshua 2; 6:17-25

What the Bible Says about Rahab

I really don't understand why some Hollywood producer has not gobbled up Rahab's story and made it a made for television movie. It is laced with the kind of drama that cuts to the very heart of survival in a changing world order. Rahab's story is a narrative built around the intrigue and conspiracy of betrayal of your own kind in order to have a better life, to survive in a new world order. This woman, a prostitute through the use of wisdom and cunning, etched out her own place in an up and coming society based on justice and freedom. Everyone in her family and in fact the entire community knew of her profession. Hers is a story of picking up the pieces of your life, no matter how broken and disconnected from what God has in store for you, and then moving on.

What did Rahab have to move on from? A prostitute is a person who provides sexual activity in exchange for material gain.[103] The parties involved are not married to each other. Prostitution in biblical imagery has also been applied to Israel, because of her self-indulgent ways which are at the heart of a prostitute.[104] Two other famous biblical women who were referred to as prostitutes are Delilah in Judges 16 and Tamar in Genesis 38. Women during Rahab's time became prostitutes by force or by choice. Young girls who had been abandoned were in some cases taken in and raised to be prostitutes. Their abusive condition made them open for grace in the valley.

Some women prostituted themselves to pagan gods or for economic reasons. These women had to actively seek forgiveness and salvation. Rahab had to change her life-style choice to gain full acceptance into God's covenant.

Rahab was probably un-churched because women of her station in life could only serve as temple prostitutes not temple worshippers. But from the deal that she made with the spies, she knew who God was and understood that she needed God's protection. The world as it was had become too much for her. She could not go on without God's help. So Rahab resolved within her heart to help God keep God's promises.

When Joshua secretly sent out two spies to determine what the Israelites would encounter when they attacked Jericho and the surrounding provinces, Rahab welcomed them into her home. The spies were probably sent out secretly because Joshua wanted to avoid the kind of dread that had fallen upon the Israelites in Moses' time as the spies returned with conflicting reports. In this instance, the help of God presupposes human action; therefore, it was not by accident that these men selected her house. Two young men entering the house of a person like her should not arouse much suspicion. However, the king's intelligence system was operating fully that day. He sent out a battalion of troops to bring the strangers in for questioning. When the king's men came knocking seeking the spies, she hid them before answering the door.

Upon greeting the soldiers, Rahab agreed that the two strangers did enter her home. She led the soldiers to believe that the men had entered for the usual purposes and she had no idea of who they were. Out of discretion, she had not asked nor was identification a requirement for persons who utilized her services. Then she goes on to say that they had left prior to the gates of the city being closed. After all, leaving at any other time would have been futile. Rahab encouraged them to follow quickly and they would be able to overtake the strangers on the road away from the city. Her quickly contrived plan worked; the soldiers left and she secured the gate behind them. Now, she was free to talk with the spies before they were able to go to sleep.

Before the spies, she bared all. Rahab had a realistic view of herself and of God. She told them that sure she was a prostitute by profession. Rahab went on to say that she believed the song of Moses and the Israelites that had been circulating around the area. She believed that the Red Sea crossing in its entire splendor, the defeat of the two kings of the Amorites, the destruction of Sihon and Og were proof that their God was the god of heaven and earth. She went on to say that God had placed dread and fear in the hearts of the Canaanites. The courage of her people to stand against God's people was dwindling day by day. God had kept his promise to Israel; the land would be theirs for the taking. Rahab's statements are a sign of faith.

In true form, she goes on to ask for something in return for her services. She wanted the men, as a result of her helping them, to swear upon an oath in the Lord's name that both Rahab and her entire family would be saved when the country was overthrown. She and the spies all agreed to the following conditions. Rahab would make her house known to the invading Israelites by tying a crimson cord to a window.[105] This was a symbolic sign of the preservation of Rahab's family's life. It is similar to the placing of the blood on the door post of the Israelites in Egypt prior to the Passover. The death angel then spared the first born of that house.

Secondly, Rahab should assemble all of her relatives into her home. This included her parents, siblings, and all persons in their individual families. If any of them were to venture outside during the battle, they would be slain at no blame of the Israelites. If the invading army were to enter her home and cause injury or death to anyone, their blood would be on the hands of Israelites. The third condition was a confirmation of the oath. If Rahab did not betray their secrets and followed the oath to the letter, she and her family would live. If either party broke the oath they would die.

The business having been settled, Rahab lets them down through the window of her house that was built into the outside wall of the city, using a crimson cord. She also gave them detailed instructions for their survival thereby helping them to make a clean getaway. The spies made it safely back to their camp. When Joshua was told of the utter despondency and alarm of the Canaanites, he was pleased. Because of Rahab's assistance, he agreed to the oath that had been made with the woman, who happened to be a prostitute. When his army moved into position for battle, Joshua confirmed the oath before the entire army.

Rahab had told a lie to protect the lives of the spies and to aid God's plan. A lie is always a sin. Rahab acted wrongly; however, the action was an exception to God only because the evil that was mixed with the good was not imputed to her. Although God did wish the spies to be delivered, God did not sanction their being protected by a lie. God could have saved them without her. Since Rahab had placed herself in such a position God did show her grace.

The battle itself had all the dynamics of a true Holy War.[106] The priest carried the Ark of the Covenant into the water to make a clear path for the Israelites to cross. It took seven days to bring down the city of Jericho. On the seventh day the Israelites moved around the city seven times. On the seventh march, the priests blew their horns, the war cry was raised. The walls crumbled before them and the city was taken. In biblical history, when Israel turned from God seeking after her own pleasures, she was referred to as a harlot. Here she is saved by a harlot.

The two spies were sent to get Rahab and her family and place them in a safe place outside of the camp of Israel. This is where they possibly remained until they had undergone the required purification rites.[107] These rites were customary at that time for acceptance into the covenant with God. Rahab embraced Judaism and later married into the tribe of Israel. As the mother of Boaz, an ancestor of David, Rahab is mentioned in the genealogy of Jesus the Christ.[108] We can appreciate Jerome's comments in his commentary, "He who came in behalf of sinners was himself born of sinners, and might destroy the sins of all."[109]She is enshrined in the faith hall of fame.[110] She is also praised along side Abraham as an example of justification through works.[111] It was her faith and obedience that saved her family.

Rahab, a common prostitute by profession, a sinner, helped the Lord to fulfill God's promise to the people of Israel. She accepted God as Lord and began living her life in a manner pleasing to God. This is what the Reverend Otis Moss, II, one of the greatest exegetical preachers of the twenty-first century terms "Redemption in a Red Light District."

Rahab: Helping a Sister Out

I am not surprised that the spies, Joshua, and even God accepted Rahab's help. The Bible is replete with examples of where God used some unlikely people. Prior to Rahab, God used Abraham, a liar who tried to prostitute his own wife, and Moses was a murderer. When we strip away the layers of her life and move past the labels that have been attached to her forehead down through history, what do we see? We see a gifted sister, a woman of great talent whose profession just happened to be prostitution.

"Prostitution is often the gateway crime for women in prison (Chesney-Lind, 1997). It has been reported that 70% of female inmates in American prisons were initially arrested for prostitution (Boyer & James, 1983, p. 131). Currently one in three women in jails today was arrested for prostitution; 7 in 10 women imprisoned for felonies were initially arrested for prostitution (Flowers, 1998, p.8)."[112]

Rahab is to be commended not for her profession or falsehood, but for her faith and the ability to negotiate and execute a contract. Prostitution is a job, a profession, a way of life. Banking was my job, my profession, my way of life. In a sense, I prostituted myself for the money, power, prestige and positions. But there is more to me than having been a banker and there is more to Rahab than being a prostitute. We engage in prostitution when we force our soul to serve our body. Looking at prostitution in that light there is probably a little bit of prostitute in each of us.

According to Nanette J. Davis, in the book, *Prostitution: An International Handbook on Trends, Problems, and Policies*, "Our status as women in today's society forces some of us to rent our bodies or stay in unsatisfying marriages."[113] I agree with her to some degree. We make deals with the landlord or the mechanic. Countless women put up with sexual harassment on the job, smile when we don't want to and put out so that we do not get fired. Then there are those of us who put on our sexiest clothes and don our makeup perfectly to obtain extra cash or the use of that credit card with the low balance. Many of us selected our mates because of their potential for earned income as opposed to the guy that was our real mate in body, mind and spirit. People who live in glass houses should never throw stones.

Prostitution is perceived by most women and by society as a whole as a poor lifestyle choice. So, what are the reasons that some women in today's society turn to professional prostitution? The same as they were back in the ancient of days, economics or oppression. And with each of these comes a laundry list of subheadings.

Some women have found themselves short on cash and lacking in the skills to maintain a "real job." So they take what is initially perceived as being the easy way out. Still others sell their bodies to keep up a drug or alcohol habit. Some women follow the road of prostitution because Mama did it. A small number of women turn to prostitution because they enjoy the work. It is done more often, because of shame or low self-image; it was something they felt they could be good at.

I am not going to discuss the full gamut of child prostitution at this juncture. However, more and more young girls in our society today are being pressured into prostitution or turned out by parents, other adults and teenage boys who see them as easy prey. These sick vultures seek to make a living off the lives of another person who is overwhelmed by the world around them or simply do not fully understand the ramifications of their actions. They keep these young girls under their power and influence by violence and material rewards. Some of the material rewards can be more easily earned by these young women taking on a part-time job. But to some young minds, it makes more sense to turn a trick for five to thirty minutes, than to work at a fast food restaurant or in some other entry level position for a few hours a day. As sisters of the Spirit, we have a responsibility to work with nonprofit and governmental agencies, the church and community to save our children.

In Christendom, we are taught to look beyond a person's faults and to see people for who they really are. Most of us are diamonds in the rough. Once you polish us up and place us in the right setting, we become more and more valuable with time and proper care. A prostitute knows how to treat a man. It is not all about sexual intercourse. A good prostitute can help a man feel whole, complete and loved even if he feels that he is only a shell of the man he once was. My sisters, there are many lessons to be learned from prostitutes about holding on to the man that God has placed at your side. The people of God are admonished to focus on the needs of sinners and saints alike, so that we can show them loving-kindness.

What can the church do for the prostitute? Many organizations have been formed to aid the victims of prostitution; some are even named in honor of Rahab. We should support a prostitute in her career change. We can assist her as we would any other person coming to our church for care when she decides that she wants to give up her habit and lifestyle choice. Love her back into submission to God and godly ways. Help her to determine what gifts she has that would be useful within the mission and ministry of the church and put her to work. Do not ostracize her. Teach her the ways of the women of God, but first some of us may need a refresher course in affirming sisterhood.

Skillfully help her with her language. When she says to you, "Your show was slamming, today and that group really got its groove on." Politely respond, "I also noticed the movement of the Holy Spirit during the worship service. The part of the sermon that blessed my heart or spoke directly to me was…By rephrasing her statement you help her to understand the purpose of the worship tradition in your setting. Every part of the worship service is an act of worship.

Worship is far more than preaching and singing praise and worship songs. It is showing adoration to our God. Everything we do to please God is also an act of worship.

When she breaks out in the 'bankhead bounce' while getting her praise on, don't condemn her to hell for dancing in the church. This woman has a lot to praise God for doing in her life. God has brought her out of darkness into God's marvelous light. God has saved her soul and provided her with a new family of loving and caring brothers and sisters. She can't help but praise the Lord. Psalm 150 reminds us it is biblical to praise the Lord in dance. And we all remember King David who danced so hard that he danced right out of his clothes. David considered it an honor to praise God in this way and the musicians pulled out all the stops on their instruments. David was not performing for the crowd. He was showing his gratitude in worship and celebrating the goodness of God to God's people. David went on to assign persons with certain skills to various positions in church worship. Today we have musicians, choir directors, ministers of music, praise teams, orchestras, percussionists, ushers, deacons, nurses, liturgists, and preachers; each playing a special role in organized worship.

If she is good at dancing and really enjoys the movement, encourage her to join the liturgical dance ministry or step team where we teach theological movement. If we don't assist others in learning the language and rituals of the church, we run the risk of not being able to differentiate between the church and the world. And, if we don't teach new babes in Christ, how will they learn and grow. We all need to understand one another, but at the same time keep God's house a house of divine worship.

Today many of our churches are walking a very thin line. Some of our worship borders on syncretism, the combination of the various beliefs and practices of organized religion with the beliefs and practices of the world. Before adopting a program or an act or service as a part of divine worship examine it to see if it has a scriptural basis or if it is honoring God. If it honors God, then we fall back on our own personal preferences and traditions as to what worship is and what worship is not. Pleasing God and not man should always be the object of worship.

I have always worked hard in the church. Because of my love for God and God's people, I prostituted my knowledge, gifts and skills to help the church move forward. My reward was at times confrontations and isolation. At other times, I received great affirmation and participation from persons who caught hold of the vision and understood that my efforts were all for the cause of Christ. If I had added two additional principles to that list: built godly alliances and used my 'spiritual wisdom' like Rahab before moving forward with projects, my road would have been easier and my rewards greater. Spiritual wisdom is more than knowledge, good sense or using good judgment or the wise use of accumulated data. It is godly insight. It is the ability to discern inner qualities and relationships. Spiritual wisdom will allow you to plan a project to complete and allow the other person to think it was their idea and then give God and them all the credit and the glory. Spiritual wisdom will keep you out of those moral mud puddles of life.

The apostle Paul was another person who did not always take the road of least resistance. He accomplished a great deal during his ministry but he did it his way and gave all the glory to the Lord. Paul talks about the grace of God in 1 Corinthians 15:10 – "But by the grace of God I am what I am, and his grace toward me has not been in vain. On the contrary, I worked harder than any of them – though it was not I but the grace of God that is with me." At times in my life, I have used what I know and used what I learned to get the job done. Now, I know better than to rely on myself alone. I have learned to rely more on the Lord to guide me through life's murky waters. I also thank God for those uncomfortable feelings that occur when I am moving in the wrong direction. They are the Spirit's reminder that I am not in this by myself. I thank God for grace and mercy when I have failed to listen. The Lord brings me through in spite of my dogmatic determination to do it my way. Redemption is refreshing and rewarding. The benefit package is out of this world.

Chapter Ten

Euodia and Syntyche: Unity within the Community of Faith Philippians 4:1-9

What the Bible Says about Euodia and Syntyche

The Philippian church was the first church Paul established on European soil. They were the jewels in his crown, a source of pride and joy. He continuously expresses his affection for them in the first half of his letter, encouraging them to be persistent in faith, even under opposition and the threat of death. He also calls upon them to live thoroughly Christian lives. Paul reminds them that "unity within the community of faith" is an essential element in a truly Christian way of living. And yet in Philippians 4:2-9, we find that there was trouble brewing in the church.

The principal parties involved in this quarrel are Euodia and Syntyche. There is little known about these women or the nature of their quarrel. The two women appear to have been important persons within the church. They were among its most active workers, perhaps within each of their homes a separate congregation met for worship. Today their homes would serve as the place where a Ward meeting, Mission Society or Bible Study group would meet.

It is clear from the numerous stories of women in ministry in the book of Acts; women played an important role in the founding and establishing of the Macedonian churches.[114]Therefore, the fact that these two women were quarreling had the potential for upsetting the harmony of the larger community of faith.

Euodia's and Syntyche's differences may have had to do with church leadership, and with which of the two women was to have the greater say within the church at Philippi. Or it could have been that one woman's personality was more prevailing thereby overshadowing the other woman's personality. There is also a similarity between these two women's argument and the quarrel that went on between the disciples in the upper room when Jesus was trying to reveal to them his passion and their future destiny. The disciples were more concerned about who would be the greatest.

Paul appeals to Euodia and Syntyche to iron out their differences and make up in a godly manner. When we examine the Greek, the verb he uses also means to implore or beg. In fact, Paul uses it twice so as to heighten its effect by repetition, and to emphasize the idea that his apostolic exhortation is made to both women equally. They each had equal responsibility for repairing their relationship. His request was for them to live harmoniously together in a way that is fit and proper for all who claim to have placed themselves under the Lordship of Christ. Paul was encouraging the women not simply to agree, but to have a common mind, identical feelings and attitudes toward each other.

These two women were to set aside the hurts that can be caused by assaults on one another's personhood. Instead of being entangled in confusion, they were to entangle each other in a web of love. Instead of exchanging rebukes, they were to show love for one another.

But Paul was also a realist; he understood how difficult it would be for Euodia and Syntyche to reach agreement on their own. So, he solicits the help of a third party. His impassioned plea to the church and its leaders was, "Help them!" He went on to say that it was the church's responsibility to bring the women together.

Paul went on to explain that the two women had worked side by side with him in the struggle to preach the gospel. With this statement, Paul affirms the fact that these women are in no way to be degraded for their disagreements. They were to be respected highly for their energetic cooperation with him while working at his side as esteemed members of the ministry team. They were Paul's coworkers equal in importance to Clement and the rest of Paul's fellow-laborers. Why their names were even inscribed in the Book of Life along with all of God's children. So it was the entire church's responsibility to promote "unity within the community of faith."

Euodia and Syntyche: Helping a Sister Out

The argument between the two women reminds me of the condition of the church today. Thousands of years after their argument, we are still clashing in the church today. There are usually three reactions when Christians clash over responsibilities or their relationships become splintered over duties in the church. You know how the scenario goes. One person says, "this is my project." The person retorts, "I am chairperson of this committee so I will have the last word on how we will handle this activity." The first reaction is for the other party to recoil. Step back, shut down and do nothing. Then the project may die. The second reaction would be to fight like the women in our text. But there is a third reaction to clashes over responsibilities, it is to unite.

Unity can lead to sharing of responsibilities and ideas. Experience and vision unite behind a common goal. There is a sense of give and take. We work and build together, each person in their own area of proficiency. There are no old timers, no new comers, no long timers, and no short timers, just church folks growing and building together.

Everyone is serving together in the presence of the Lord. We develop a partnership in our mission, in our ministry, and in our relationship with one another. We can safely surmise from the text that this third response, unity, is what Paul was striving to accomplish by calling the church's attention to the dispute between the two women.

On those occasions when you have to resolve conflict, remember that conflict is not a win-lose situation. The goal should be to arrive at a solution that is acceptable to all parties. Do not criticize; be helpful with your comments. Forgive, no matter what comes out during the discussion. You cannot read another person's mind, don't jump to conclusions. Allow them to share their feelings. We are to practice careful listening and strive not to be judgmental. Restate their comments to be sure of what you think you heard. I know that it is difficult, but try not to hang on to the past. It is a big person who is willing to admit that you may have contributed to the problem through error or omission. Describe your own feelings in a constructive way. If the other person is unable to hear what you are saying, it may be best to reschedule your meeting. Do not assign guilt if things don't go smoothly the first time around. Focus on a solution not on the problem. If the conflict has multiple layers, deal with them one by one. Then, let it go! Let it go! Let It Go!

The further implication for us today is it takes two to keep a dispute going. Accept a person's right to disagree as long as they are not disagreeable. If they become disagreeable, rather than denigrate or stereotype them, be compassionate, professional, assertive and yet willing to 'help a sister or a brother out.' When the church closes her eyes to antagonist and antagonistic situations, in the hope that they will settle things among themselves or it will just go away; we run the risk of others being pulled into their disputes. Disputes are like infections. The infection will spread and an infected wound may cause gangrene to occur. Then radical steps will need to be taken. Let us not wait to perform radical surgery when a little care and a little attention, a little antiseptic and daily cleansing with prayer, can prevent the loss of a limb from the body of Christ. An ounce of prevention is truly worth more than a pound of cure.

As we take a closer look at the text, we find that Paul did not rely on his own knowledge of the situation and conflict strategy alone; he reminds the women and the entire congregation that Christ is going to return to claim his church. Then Paul lays out a plan of action when trouble comes tugging at the heartstrings of the body of Christ. He shares four imperatives that will help us to maintain "unity within the community of faith."

First, rejoice in the Lord always. This implies that the joy of the Christian is not a passing fancy. Rejoicing is not to be reserved for special times of worship or praise. It is to be uninterrupted and unbroken. Paul and Silas while locked away in prison chose to rejoice and began the first revival in the prison system. African-American people chose to rejoice while bound by the shackles of slavery and the African-American Church took root in this nation. In spite of annoyances, disagreements, and persecutions, our lives are to be one continuous period of rejoicing.

Coupled with the undaunted joy of rejoicing, the apostle urges us to show godly gentleness in our interactions with one another. Our way of relating is shaped by the fast-paced world in which we live, a world of assertiveness, bluntness, curtness, and presumption. Some of us live by the motto: I will get you before you can get me. Or, hurt me and I'll hurt you back. Gentleness is no soft virtue. It is a character quality that controls our capacity for rage and activates our capacity to love. Gentle people are courteous, kind, exercise restraint, and practice reticence in speech. They know that words can wound and silence may be more affirming than chatter. Gentle people are happy people.

The third way to promote unity in the community is by not being anxious about anything. More accurately put, stop worrying! This no pious cliché or easy moralizing about complex issues. We must consider the circumstance out of which Paul's letter comes, he was in prison. Paul's words come from the sweaty arena of life and it is within the sweaty arena of our lives that his words need to be heard. His words come from a person who had experienced the answer that he is offering.

The alternative to worry is Paul's fourth point. Paul urges us to pray, believing that God is greater than the greatest problem and that God is the rewarder of those who earnestly seek him.[115] We can find release from anxiety through prayer and more prayer. He learned during his difficult lifetime to pray about everything. He admonished the church to let God know what was on their mind, as if God needed to be informed.[116] This is but the apostle's quaint way of expressing the very personal nature of prayer.

And he closed that section of the letter with these words, "Whatever is true, honorable, just, pure, pleasing, commendable, if anything is excellent or praiseworthy; think about such things and put them into practice. And the God of peace will be with you."[117] So, my sisters, it is time we stopped buying into all those negative stereotypes out there about women not being able to work together. Reflect and remember all of the things that are being accomplished daily by women in the workplace and look around you in the church. Who is it that is doing all of the actual hands-on-ministry in the church? If you look for negatives you will surely find them. We are to focus on the positives in life; think the best of people.

Chapter Eleven

Mary Magdalene: Blessed to be a Witness
Luke 8:1-3; 24:1-12;
Matthew 26:57; 27:61; 28:1-10;
Mark 15:40, 47; 16:1-9; John 19:25;
John 20:1-18

What the Bible Says about Mary Magdalene

Mary called Magdalene is believed to have come from Magdala, a prosperous fishing village on the Sea of Galilee between Tiberias and Capernaum. The name magdala means tower and we will soon learn that Mary lived up to her name 'tower.' She is mentioned fourteen times in the gospels. She was a recipient of Jesus' saving grace and delivering hand.[118]

In Mary Magdalene's story, we see what Jesus the Christ is able to do for a deeply troubled woman. Her first name means rebellion. This afflicted woman's body was hostess to seven demons. These demons can be characterized as evil agents that were the source of great harm and distress. In reading her story we can't really put our finger on any one thing that would unveil for us the totality of her problem. Persons who have been identified as being demon possessed or having evil spirits are sometimes mislabeled because they exhibit signs and symptoms that we do not fully understand. The Bible teaches us that among its many manifestations demons would cause mental disorder, violent action, bodily disease, and rebellion against God.[119] Their condition may manifest itself in extreme forms of psychological, sociological and physiological behavior.[120]

One can only imagine the havoc that these spirits wreaked in her house. Seven, the mystic number meaning complete, leads us to believe her possession was extremely severe. The Bible does not inform us of what weakened state she may have been in that made her an easy target for demons to attack. She may have had a chemical imbalance, suffered from depression, or simply have been ill when they entered and took up full residence within her body, mind, and spirit. What we do know is they met their match when Jesus, under the power of the Spirit of God, banished them from her body.[121] Jesus during his ministry performed many exorcisms and withstood the demon position in his own life circumstances. Exorcism was a part of his divine calling.[122]

After her healing, Mary believed there was nothing that Jesus could not do. She knew from experience that he could heal your body. He could cure your diseases. He could cast out demons. Every time she saw Jesus, thought about Jesus, considered what she had been through, her soul cried Halleluiah. But, not just her soul, I can imagine she hollered, "I'm Free! I'm Free! Thank God, I'm Free!"

Having been delivered from so much, no woman or man surpasses Mary Magdalene in her devotion to Jesus. She was so grateful to be rid of all she had experienced. She became a faithful member of his entourage, those persons who accompanied him from city to city. Clothed and in her right mind, Mary Magdalene became an eyewitness on the front lines during Jesus' miracle crusades.

Following her healing, Mary began to put her faith into action. She was a woman of means so she helped to support Jesus' ministry out of her own resources.[123] She was one of the witnesses present at the cross during the most important event in history, the crucifixion of Jesus. She was standing at the foot of the cross with Jesus' mother and aunt when

Jesus asked the beloved disciple to take his mother, Mary, into his care and treat her as his own mother.[124] How her heart must have ached when Jesus gave a loud cry and breathed his last breath.[125]

As Joseph of Arimathea took Jesus' bloody, mangled, broken, lifeless body and hurriedly placed it in his new tomb, Mary was there looking on. She saw where his body was laid. She then remained at the tomb with Jesus' aunt long after all the other mourners had gone home.[126] She simply could not believe Jesus had gone out like this. He did so much good and now he had died like a common criminal. I imagine she could not sleep at all that night. She kept replaying the events of his life in her head. She reflected on all that he had said to her and to the other disciples. Now all the riddles were beginning to make sense.

On the first day of the week in the pre-dawn hours as the sun lifted its head over the horizon, Mary could be seen hurrying through the garden. Mary knew that she would have to confront the soldiers who had been placed at the front of the tomb. She did not know how she would remove the huge boulder from the mouth of the tomb. In addition to these obstacles, she was placing her own life in jeopardy by being associated with Jesus. In spite of all these odds against her, this devoted disciple went back to the tomb to anoint Jesus' body so that he would have a proper Jewish burial. Surely, doing this would bring her some consolation.

As she arrived at the tomb, an earthquake shook the ground under her feet. She regained her composure enough to look up and see an angel descending from heaven. He rolled the stone away from the opening to the tomb. The guards were petrified with fear. They just stood there shaking in their boots. As she gazed into the empty tomb, Jesus' body had escaped without the linen wrappings being unwound. The cloth which had been wrapped about his head lay apart still rolled up. His body was missing. Jesus was not there.

The angel spoke to her and told her that Jesus had been raised from the dead and had left a message for her. She was to go and tell his disciples that he had gone ahead of them to Galilee. Mary becomes the first human to be entrusted with the awesome responsibility of sharing the message of Christ's resurrection. Both terror and amazement seized her. She left the tomb excited, moved by fear and great joy. She ran to give the good news to the disciples. [127]

Jesus met her and said, Greetings! Then she bowed down, took hold of his feet and began to worship him. [128] This was another first for this woman, others were told not to touch his body. As Mary stood there weeping, Jesus told her, "Do not be afraid, go tell my brothers I'll meet them in Galilee."[129] The last to leave the cross, the first to return to the tomb, this woman was the vessel Jesus chose to announce his resurrection to the disciples. Mary Magdalene had now become a strong tower (the meaning of the second part of her name). So she told the disciples all that he had said. All these things were shared to evoke belief in Jesus the Christ as the Messiah.

And yet, the disciples did not believe. They were convinced of the truth of Jesus' resurrection only by their own immediate experience with him. Although, they should have heeded the witness of Mary Magdalene, as we should also do today. Christ is alive and we too will be called up to meet him someday. In the meantime, we are to take a page from Mary's book; seek help, trust and believe. Once we are healed of those things that block our view of God, we are to give our best in service.

Mary Magdalene: Helping a Sister Out

Mary Magdalene, a woman whose picture is often symbolized in sacred art along with Mary the mother of Jesus and other devout women, is an outstanding example of the spirits of service and stewardship. Before she took on her full status in the ministry, she took the time to be healed of her demons. Her first example for us today is to get professional help for our 'conditions;' those annoying things that we know cause us to be dysfunctional. This woman, whose life was blessed so richly by Jesus, gave it all back in body, mind and spirit. She was probably a single woman of independent means because she was free to travel with Jesus from place to place and to give financial support to his ministry. She was a disciple in waiting. After fulfilling her appointed role, Jesus elevated her to full status. Through an angel of God, she was ordained to be the first disciple to share the resurrection story.

Following her example, we too should give our very best in service. We are to share of our time and resources with those who have been called to be apostles, prophets, evangelist, pastors and teachers.[130] During the first part of her ministry she was an armor bearer for the Lord.

An armor bearer is an anointed and appointed person who is the guardian of those items necessary for a leader to share in the ministry. This person looks after the personal needs of the leader while they are serving the people of God. They are first anointed by God for service and later identified by a leader and appointed to serve in the capacity of armor bearer. Some of the qualities and duties of an armor bearer that I share in my workshops are included here. A loyal, trustworthy, pleasant, professional and confidential armor bearer can be one of God's greatest gifts to a person in the ministry. Armor bearers' spiritual gifts include but are not limited to one or more of the following: service, helps, hospitality and intercessory prayer.

To be a successful armor bearer one must learn how to do it. There are several very good books on the subject and most churches have guidelines for serving the leadership. The key thing to remember is that servanthood is a sacred duty. Your duties are to be carried out without concern or desire for position, popularity or recognition. Your duties may run the gamut from carrying the leader's Bible to driving her home at the end the day. You not only help the leader when you drive them from place to place but you may wish to drop their robe at the cleaners or pick up bottled water or juice to keep handy should the congregation where they are serving fail to have some on hand. Some armor bearers do research for the leader, as well. Clarify your duties with the person you are to serve or with the person in charge of armor bearers. If your church or leader does not have specific guidelines to share with you over a period of time you may assist them in developing a job description for armor bearers. Always remember flexibility is a key element in your job duties.

Armor bearers who possess the spiritual gift of hospitality are great around strangers. They are very welcoming and affirming of the persons who want to get close to the leader. They act as greeters assisting the leader when they are swamped by worshippers at the close of a service. They create unity. A hospitable person does not come between the leader and the people they are called to serve. Extend certain courtesies to the spouse of the person you have been called to serve. Remember their spouse is their helpmate, the person who has been chosen by God to stand at their side and to share in their ministry.

Get to know the person you have been called to serve. This will mean studying them while they are performing their ministry duties and while they are at rest. Invite them out at your expense as an act of kindness and fellowship. Learn their likes, dislikes and idiosyncrasies. When you get to know a leader through their work, as a fellow human being and as the person who has charge over you, a mutual respect will develop. You will esteem them highly in love because of their work.[131]

The leader's armor bearer is a very confidential person. They do not share their weaknesses with others; this may cause them to fall away. You are to check yourself periodically and make sure you are modeling Christian behavior. Bear in mind that no one is perfect. We are all striving to maintain a pure heart and a right spirit.[132] The person you serve has a direct communication with God. They should be leading a godly life, setting a good example and sharing sound doctrine. And if you are also hearing from God, you should be blessed to be a part of their ministry.[133]

Apostles, prophets, evangelists, pastors and teachers are some of the most prayed for people on earth. Think about it, every time they stand before God's people everyone is praying for them. Jesus himself is whispering words of endearment into the ear of God on their behalf. Therefore, you should also pray continuously for the person you have been called and appointed to serve. Become their intercessor before the Lord. And do not fail to pray for yourself. This is how you both gain strength and blessings for the journey. It was Paul who penned these words, "Finally, brothers and sisters, pray for us, so that the word of the Lord may spread rapidly and be glorified everywhere, just as it is among you."[134] Being an armor bearer is a high calling. If you choose to accept this mission assignment, there will be times that you will bend low before God lifts you up.

Chapter Twelve

Eve: A Costly Decision
Genesis 1- 4

What the Bible Says about Eve

Some biblical scholars say that Eve was given life because God wanted a more intelligent creation to manage the earth on God's behalf. Others go with the theory that God could not find a suitable companion for the man so he created woman. I agree with the group that says both theories, being supported by scripture, are correct. Therefore, I cannot share details of Eve's story without including Adam. Genesis 1 gives us an overview of the sequential order of the creation events, while Genesis 2 returns to the creation of humankind to give us more vivid details. As we peer into the mind of God through the aid of the biblical text, we learn that it was by God's design and desire that humankind, male and female, be actual images of God. It is because we are like God that we have the capacity for fellowship with God and for meaningful relationships with each other.

The man was made from the dust of the ground. God breathed into his nostrils the breath of life. A suitable companion for the man could not be found among God's other creations. So God performed the first recorded surgical procedure; removing a rib from the man's side. God made woman. Woman was created by God to be the man's helpmate not his foot mat. She was born of a rib from his side, this means she should always be close to his heart. His arm should always enfold her and protect her. She is to stand at his side not ahead or behind him. She is to be his companion and partner.

Eve and Adam were exalted above all other living things. God was so pleased with humankind that he termed everything that had been made before them as good, but when referring to the man and the woman, they were described as being 'very good.' It was at this juncture that we realize humankind corresponds perfectly to God's intentions. To be made in the image of God means that you take on God's characteristics and God's likeness in relationship and activities. So God gave them dominion over everything that God had made. Together man and woman were to share the task of being God's stewards of the earth. Humankind was commissioned to manage God's rule on the earth.

In the Garden of Eden humankind had everything they needed. The garden was designed for habitation and to encourage full development of human potential. There was beauty to encourage humankind's aesthetic capacities. There were natural resources to use. There were opportunities for them to exercise their own creative abilities and meaningful work to do. And they had each other to share in all the good gifts of God.[135] However, God commanded the man not to eat of the tree of the knowledge of good and evil or he would surely die. Adam shared this warning with Eve.

Adam and Eve begin living in the garden as husband and wife. And marriage was instituted as a divine ordinance. God was no absentee landlord, God could be found walking in the garden in the cool of the day. There was beauty, peace and tranquility in the garden.

It was a satanic serpent who brought chaos into the garden and started the ball of sin rolling. Satan's (the spirit inside the serpent) strategy was to drive a wedge of doubt between God and humankind. So God's word was questioned and contradicted. His motives were denied.

When Eve fell prey to the slick talking serpent, she underwent a transferral[136] of spirit; she set aside confidence in God's wisdom and love for greed, sensory pleasure and position.[137] She gave to him her innocence and virtue. She took on the spirit of the world,[138] earthly wisdom and concerns that stand in contrast to the wisdom and gifts given by God. Eve made a costly decision to reach for the unknown and Adam jumped on the bandwagon. Eve's decision affected God's relationship with humankind for an eternity. Adam's decision just like Eve's was an exercise of freewill. Their decision to defy God brought sin into the garden and into the lives of humankind.

Adam and Eve were crushed by guilt and shame. They hid from God afraid of their creator. When God confronted them knowing full well what they had done. They shifted the blame from one to the other trying to justify themselves. They accused and excused. Their sinful actions caused disharmony and robbed them of inner peace. Adam and Eve lost fellowship with God.

After God had heard enough of their feeble excuses, God dispenses justice in the form of rhythmical curses.[139] The serpent's form would change and he would be afflicted by humankind. Eve would have increased labor pains and struggle during childbirth. The relationship between Eve and her husband would be one of a struggle for domination. Rather than the earth being subdued by Adam, there would now be a struggle against nature. Adam would have to work much harder before the earth would yield her increase. And all creation would groan until a day comes when the curse would be removed. And to avoid further damage to God's created order, Adam and Eve were banished from the garden forever. The impact for them is both moral and psychological. The curses placed upon Adam and Eve by God became each of our lot to bear.[140]

The first family became a dysfunctional unit. Brother turned against brother. Their son, Cain, out of jealousy kills his brother Abel. Their sins multiplied and death cast a dark shadow over the face of the earth. I am happy to say, all was not lost. Their story does end with a ray of hope. One of Cain's descendants was the father of all who play the harp and flute. It is through his line that we get the first musical instruments played by humankind.

Eve gave birth to three sons; it was through her third son Seth's child, Enosh that regular divine worship was instituted and humankind began to "call on the name of the Lord."[141] It was also through his bloodline that Noah descended and the human family was preserved through the flood. Sometimes future generations have to redeem the family because of costly decisions made during past generations. This was the case with Eve's prodigy.[142] Eve's story should be a reminder to each of us that we cannot change the past, but we can make better decisions for ourselves in the future.

Eve: Helping a Sister Out

"Deliver Us From Eva"[143] is a 2003 movie that has a theological message that dates back to the time of Adam and Eve. In the movie, Eva's sisters' mates devised a scheme to separate the younger sisters from Eva's overpowering influence and the family fortune. They hired a handsome young man named Ray with little integrity to seduce the older sister. Eva was too busy being 'Eva' to notice or care about what the men thought about her.

Once she succumbed to Ray's charm, there was a transferral of spirits. Just as the serpent or Satan deceived Eve in the Garden of Eden, the young man in this movie deceived Eva. Eva, the polished professional and practicing Christian became this slang-speaking, fornicating, fun-loving person, while he developed a conscience and began singing in the choir at church. When the truth came out she was hurt and they both felt ashamed and guilty. Since he also took on her spirit, we were led to believe that they got things right in the end.

We too can be led astray from a sincere and pure devotion to Christ to a life of sin.[144] As Christians when we exercise our freewill by taking on the character of the world, which can be a costly decision, we have undergone a transferral of spirits.

Sometimes, we do this by marrying the wrong mate. You are saved and you know that he is unsaved. You begin living in the fast lane just to hold his attention. You keep telling yourself; he really isn't that bad. He didn't have a father figure in his life; he will change one day. Or you are going to convince him to make a change for the good. While you are playing these games with your own mind, you are only fooling yourself. One morning you may wake up to find that you have become this person that you don't even recognize. And he is still doing the same old things. We cannot change another person. They must want to change and that change must come from within.

Some couples practice marriage, shack up so long that marriage becomes a non-issue. It is true that marriage does begin when two hearts unite as one but there should also be a civil/religious ceremony and covenant involved. Marriage is a sacred union between a man and a woman. Also some persons have begun to defy God by entering into same sex unions. They do this under the guise that they are persons who have a right to make decisions about their own personal sexual preferences. Yes, they do have the same freewill as those of us who choose to follow God's divine design for marriage. However, God's word should not be manipulated to justify our sins. My Bible says and I believe that marriage was created for companionship and procreation between a man and a woman.

Another costly decision we make is to fall in love with our jobs at the expense and to the neglect of our families. When a mother who has a small child chooses to spend excessively long hours at work or go back to school while holding down a full-time job, she is missing out on an important period in the life of her child. This mother will miss precious moments that can never be reclaimed. No video camera image can replay the excitement or replace the joy between a parent and a child during moments of discovery. Some events will be lost forever. Sometimes, we work overtime or go back to school so that we can increase our ability to care for our families. Other times it is a way of escape. Whatever the underlying factor, we must each count the cost.

At other times, we choose to live above our means bringing financial disaster upon our household. Our wants begin to outweigh our needs and the stress of making $5000 in monthly household income cover $6000 in fixed household expenses, not including our discretionary spending, can cause most marriages to blow up in our face.

So, what is the moral of the story? How do we handle these costly decisions? We are to follow the precepts and examples of God as outlined in the world's best selling book, the Bible. Never forget that the Lord has our best interest at heart. Consult the Lord before making questionable decisions. Never make a long-range decision while you are upset or under pressure. Pray over it. Write it down and pray over it again.

Once we realize that things in our life have gotten away from God's divine design,[145] we have made the first step in redeeming our life situation. The next step is to confess all before God, ask for forgiveness and help. Accept God's forgiveness. Walk in God's ways,[146] remembering that we bear the image and likeness of God. This is a statement about our personhood. Sin has not robbed us of our personhood or of the potential for fellowship with God.

One of Satan's tactics is to play the 'Shame Game' with us. He did it with Eve and Adam. He has done it with me and he can do it with you. I have learned to enjoy and utilize the 'Shame Game' for my good. Out of shame, Eve and Adam covered themselves in the Garden of Eden with leaves. But look what God did. God covered them with the skins of animals. God shed blood in the garden to cover the sins of the 'first couple.' God covered them in their shame. We are only human; our human experiences are always vulnerable to violation.[147] We need protection.

Some of us take on shame inappropriately. We become ashamed after being raped, ashamed of being poor, ashamed of relatives who sin and the list goes on. We are not to accept the sins of another person or group and bear them as our cross. That was Jesus' role. The great shame of innocence being annihilated on the cross not only underscores the horror of sin and the judgment of God but it also offers the glory of forgiveness and restoration to all who have sinned. If you have no sense of shame you are more apt to sin. If you have a healthy sense of shame you will not usually sin quickly before the Lord.

God's covering was the first step in forgiveness for the 'First Couple.' That same covering that God gave Eve and

Adam is extended to each of us through the 'blood death' of Jesus Christ on the cross at Calvary.

We have worth and value. There is some good in each of us. We do have the potential for restoration. Accept the free gift of salvation in Christ.[148] We have been bought with a price. Christ died for my sins and your sins. Salvation is within your grasp.

I choose to draw from life every ounce of everything that God has appointed for me. But I make my decisions by first utilizing spiritual wisdom and then common sense. This was a difficult lesson for me to learn. I had to bump my head (make mistakes) many times before I learned to count the cost of my decisions. In church lore, the fruit that Eve unwisely consumed is pictured as an apple. The first thing I ever stole was an apple from the neighborhood store when I was hungry. The reason I stole the apple was unimportant to my older sister who was with me and to my mother. My sister was terribly embarrassed by my actions and my mother was ashamed of my actions. The more she beat me the harder I cried and the more she cried. Mother eventually forgave me as did the store owner but I had to pay a price for my decision to steal. Because I admitted to my sin and asked for forgiveness, the store owner later gave me a job cleaning up around the store. He never watched me or mentioned my thievery again. Remember, you will one day pay the price if you take an apple from the neighborhood store without getting permission from the owner. But, if you sincerely regret your poor choice and ask forgiveness, the store owner will work with you and you can start over with a clean slate. We call it grace.

Chapter Thirteen

Extraordinary Me: An Unwritten Book

Now Jesus did many other signs in the presence of his disciples which are not written in this book. But these are written so that you may come to believe that Jesus is the Messiah, the Son of God, and that through believing you may have life in his name. ~ John 20:30

At this point, I feel much like John must have felt when he penned these words near the end of his Gospel. God has opened my eyes to so much around me that this small book cannot contain it all. I have struggled for days trying to be obedient to the Spirit and sharing as the Lord opens up the portals of my mind. What shall I pass on to women who are hurting and in need of healing? What do I pass on to women who are searching for their divine purpose? What do I pass on to women who are already in touch with the Creator and Sustainer of life and are simply reading this book for spiritual rejuvenation? Then this melody began to play itself out in my consciousness, "I come to the garden alone, while the dew is still on the roses; and the voice I hear, falling on my ear, the Son of God discloses."[149] So I share within the lines of this chapter more of myself. I share insights from my own personal struggle as I have with women that God has allowed me to minister one on one with down through the years. As I thought about it, God has always used me and my story to – help a sister out. So I rested quietly and allowed the Spirit to center my thoughts on that which would be food for your spirits. I was led to Psalm 139.

Psalm 139

O Lord, you have searched me and known me,
You know when I sit down and when I rise up;
You discern my thoughts from far away.
You search out my path and my lying down,
And are acquainted with all my ways.
Even before a word is on my tongue,
O Lord, you know it completely.
You hem me in, behind and before,
And lay your hand upon me.
Such knowledge is too wonderful for me;
It is so high that I cannot attain it.

Where can I go from your spirit?
Or where can I flee from your presence?
If I ascend to heaven, you are there;
If I make my bed in Sheol, you are there.
If I take the wings of the morning and settle
At the farthest limits of the sea,
Even there your hand shall lead me,
And your right hand shall hold me fast.
If I say, "Surely the darkness shall cover me,
And the light around me become night,"
Even the darkness is not dark to you;
The night is as bright as the day,
For darkness is as light to you.

For it was you who formed my inward parts;
You knit me together in my mother's womb.
I praise you, for I am fearfully and wonderfully made.
Wonderful are your works;
That I know very well.

My frame was not hidden from you,
When I was being made in secret,
Intricately woven in the depths of the earth.
Your eyes beheld my unformed substance.
In your book were written all the days
That were formed for me,
When none of them as yet existed.
How weighty to me are your thoughts, O God!
How vast is the sum of them!
I try to count them –they are more than the sand;
I come to the end – I am still with you.

O that you would kill the wicked, O God,
And that the bloodthirsty would depart from me –
Those who speak of you maliciously,
And lift themselves up against you for evil!
Do I not hate those who hate you, O Lord?
And do I not loathe those who rise up against you?
I hate them with perfect hatred;
I count them my enemies.
Search me, O God, and know my heart;
Test me and know my thoughts.
See if there is any wicked way in me,
And lead me in the way everlasting.
Amen

I have used this Psalter for personal devotions on many occasions. It is also the scripture I use to introduce persons to walking the Labyrinth. I was first introduced to this Psalter by one of my seminary professors in a course called Foundations for Ministry. We were instructed to read the psalm daily and to record our thoughts in a journal for the length of that course. This Psalter is much more than a prayer for deliverance from personal enemies. It is a prayer that allows you to bare all before the Lord and become as intimate with God today as you were the day you were born.

This is also a prayer for God to examine our heart and to see our true devotion. Everything that we do, have ever done or thought is known to God. No matter where we find ourselves on any given day of the week, every moment in time, God is with us. God knew us before we were a twinkle in our parent's eyes. God knew us before we were ever conceived. God has known our character from the time of our conception until this very hour. God has not brought judgment down upon us. God is patiently waiting for us to return to the one who loves us the most, our lover, our very best friend and our guide.

During my first four months with this Psalter, I took a journey back to my childhood and meditated on all the things that my mother had shared with me regarding my birth narrative. I was able to walk with God and observe my life journey from birth through adolescence, through the teens years, young adulthood and the big five zero. As time went on, I was able to uncover all those subconscious thoughts that I needed to utter in God's presence. God and I relived the good and the bad times. I recalled being pampered as a toddler, raped as a child, beaten up by older kids, abandoned by my parents (They did not look at it as abandonment.), encouraged by a community who saw things in me that I could not see in myself, being married to a man who was trying to find his identity by dominating a clueless child, going to the church for help and being given the worst possible advice, marrying and re-marrying until I finally got it right, being called into the ministry and being rejected by Christians, struggling to make sense of a God who blesses you to suffer, then picks you up and propels you forward on the wings of a dove, experiencing the jubilation of knowing that you were God's vessel that helped a dying soul see God's great light.

God has not missed a chapter in our lives. The Lord knows our every thought, action, need and desire. God is simply waiting on us to get in step with him so that our every step can become a part of our divine purpose. In order to catch up to where God wanted me to be I had to open before the Lord all of my secret wounds for cleansing and binding up. I entered God's presence poverty stricken and I now walk with the Lord as a woman of substance. When you fully experience God as omniscient-all knowing, omnipresent – always present, and omnipotent – all power-ful you are ready to walk with God into your eternal destiny. My journey during that time period is an unwritten autobi-ography. My life story is capsuled in daily journals that I pull out and reflect on when I feel myself getting weary.

After those four months were over, I was in a place of perfect peace. I never felt closer to the Lord. I wanted to stay right where I was with God. For me time could have stopped at that moment. But the Spirit released me to go forward in the grace of the Lord. That is when I became *'A Servant on the Way...'* This phrase has become my motto and will become my epitaph. Everything that has happened to me in life was a part of God's divine plan for my life or it happened within God's permissive will. That is why I have been able to endure so much. I have trusted in God and God has never failed me yet.

Extraordinary Me: Helping a Sister Out

Your life is also an unwritten book. God has not fin-ished with you yet. Each day the Spirit is proving and refining you until that great day. I encourage you to reflect upon this Psalm 139 during your times of personal devotion for at least seven days or longer and take note of what God speaks into your spirit. Keep a journal. What do your pages of your unwritten book say? This Psalter when read prayerfully will allow you to experience God as your loving Creator and Sustainer. It allows you to open up all those hidden places before the Lord so that you can be at peace.

The Psalter is divided into four parts. Part I, verses one through six is a profession of God's knowledge of the psalmist. In part II, verses seven through twelve he confesses that God is inescapable. God is acknowledged as creator, sustainer and time keeper in part III, verses thirteen through eighteen. And lastly, in the concluding verses nineteen through twenty-four, the psalmist professes a zealous loyalty to God and holds himself up before the Lord for divine judgment. It is no light matter to be examined by God. When I traveled this journey for the first time I was filled with guilt, anxiety and at times I felt depraved. It was at these low moments that God would speak to me and lift me out of my self-pity and into spiritual bliss.

Some commentators say that Psalm 139 is a prayer for God to look into your heart and to see your true devotion. When God does this God also examines your life and your very soul. Before you can be spiritually healed you must know yourself for who and what you are, a sinner. In that God knows us and searches our very essence. Our all-knowing God can also clean us up and straighten us out. God can make us whole. After reading each set, sit quietly before the Lord. Listen and follow the leading of the Spirit. Make notes in your journal at each point where you feel the movement of the Spirit across the altar of your heart.

At the close of the seventh day, take a few minutes to pray. Then make a list of your weaknesses and a separate list of your strengths, the things that you are good at. Some of us are so modest that we fail to acknowledge our strengths and abilities. If you are an excellent manager or cook, claim it in Jesus' name. It is not boasting. It is acknowledging the gifts and skills that God has blessed you with and putting them to work for God's divine purposes. Make another list of your passions, the things that you enjoy doing more than anything else. Your passions are those things that you feel called to do and you are also good at them.

Your weaknesses are those areas where you need God's help the most. They are the things that can block your anointing. Another way to view your weaknesses is as limitations. If you are an introvert, you prefer working alone. Do not seek a job or position in the ministry that requires you to work as a part of a group in order to be effective. Your limitation is no longer a limitation when you recognize and move beyond it. So be honest with yourself. If you can't carry a tune and you are in the choir that is a limitation. Use your limitations as stepping stones that propel you onward to a place and position where God can use you. God wants your best in service. Pray for deliverance in these areas of weakness. Compare your strengths and passions. How can you utilize your strengths and passions in God's service? Pray about it.

I caution you to take your time. In most of your cases, it took years for you to get where you are today. It will take some time for you to get where God wants you to be. One day at a time is sufficient for the Lord. You are a work in progress. If God were to answer all of your prayers or to change your life with a 'poof' there would be no need for faith. God's seeming delay to the answering of your prayers and the changing of your life's circumstances simply requires that you remain patient and faithful. Keep something constructive constantly going on in your life. When you are faithful in your relationships, commitments and in prayer, the Spirit will intercede for you and work things out for your good.[150]

Recently, we observed the second anniversary of one of the worst days in modern history, September 11 or '911.' The news commentator showed the progress being made at Ground Zero. I wondered why the work was going so slow. After discussing the matter with a friend who is an engineer, he told me that the Twin Towers were built over a landfill. If they hurriedly remove the debris from 911, it may cause instability in the earth below and the area may collapse. Then there would be more chaos. Therefore, the work has to go one level at a time under the supervision of a structural engineer.

Our lives are a lot like Ground Zero. Many of us are walking around today on broken pieces. If that is your situation, I recommend that you get in touch with your structural engineer. His name is Jesus. He knows every hair on your head. His spirit is with you when you rise up and when you lay down. Using him as your guide, take time and survey your life's circumstances to determine the degree of devastation. Then begin stripping away all the debris in your life, one layer at a time; putting support systems in place as you go along. Your support systems include prayer, the Word of God, a healthy lifestyle, realistic goals and objectives, family, personal friends and the community of faith. However, if you have several issues or 'a condition' that is preventing you from being whole, no 'how to' book is going to solve or resolve your problem. Books often help us to face the fact that we do have a problem. Books often help to give us that little nudge or added strength to take

God's hand and move on to the next step. For many of us that next step is to seek the services of a trained professional. There are three people who can move you along the road to wholeness: God, Extraordinary You, and the trained professional that you open up to. However, you must be willing to move forward in faith, nothing wavering. Ask your Senior Pastor, Pastor for Membership Nurture and Care, Health Ministry Leader, Physician, or a 'friend in recovery' for a referral to a professional. Select the professional you feel comfortable with and ask God to help you to participate fully with that person to effect your healing. If you listen to the Lord's prompting your body will be healed, restored and resurrected to new life. I encourage you to try God's way and enjoy the journey...

Epilogue

OUR ENDINGS ARE GOD'S BEGINNING

Psalm 126:5-6 says, *"May those who sow in tears reap with shouts of joy. Those who go out weeping, **bearing** the seed for sowing, shall come home with shouts of joy, carrying their sheaves. "* This text epitomizes what happened to me during my sabbatical or 40-Day Journey of Intimacy with God. I went out empty and returned full. God granted me grace in the valley. Now that I look at this text, I thought I was empty but I had all of this love and spiritual power inside of me crying to come out, longing to be set free. My seeds are the many gifts, talents and skills that God has so graciously lavished upon me. I have been holding my own potential a prisoner inside of me. My seeds are sprouting. It is now time to transplant the new growth so that God's people can reap an even greater harvest through my work for the Lord.

This book began because I was a woman in search of my divine purpose in life. It was there in front of me all along. I have been living out my divine purpose in every sermon that I have ever preached. God has accomplished great things through me in every workshop that I conducted under "ELS Ministries" which seeks to empower God's people to go into all settings, both sacred and secular, bringing healing and restoration to a broken people. The Lord has healed and resurrected the people of God through my "Power of God for The Woman in the Mirror Conferences," helping women to experience the power of God in their life in new ways. And God's divine purpose for me was evidenced in the administrative and managerial work carried out through "The Mission Institute and Your Choice Center, Inc.," a faith-based nonprofit organization which empowers persons with life-changing skills for self-sufficiency while revitalizing communities. I have been privileged to do some awesome work for the Lord. These three areas of my ministry will now come under one umbrella. Thanks be to God!

Sunday, September 21, 2003

Sometimes God does not fully answer all of our prayers in the midst of our time of spiritual reflection. That's why I always try to remain in God's presence. I woke up the Sunday following my forty-day journey of intimacy with God, at one o'clock in the morning. God would not allow me to rest. I felt a need to listen to the Lord speak. The words started coming so clear and fast. I knew a sermon was being birthed in my mind and in my heart. So I turned on the light and took hold of my pen and pad and penned the words of this sermon. It was the conclusion that I had been waiting on for my book. But in the midst of my joy and tears, I soon learned that it was the conclusion of another leg of my journey in the Lord's service and the beginning of a new road into ministry.

NOW IS THE ACCEPTABLE TIME

Luke 4:18-19

Having come out of a wilderness place where he had been tempted by Satan, Jesus realizing his divine purpose traveled around for about a year teaching in various synagogues. Before he had made a public proclamation of the course his ministry was to take, Jesus was already working in his calling. On this particular occasion, he had returned to Nazareth in Galilee, the town where he grew up.[151]

Early on in his ministry, Jesus had developed a practice of participating in public worship. This is an example for those of us who are called to positions of leadership in the ministry. We are to maintain our fellowship with the saints through opportunities for corporate worship where we are not in charge. Today many pastors and evangelists speak of it as "covering." You have a pastor's pastor that you confide in and a congregation that is family. They pray your strength in the Lord and for the ministry that God has assigned to your hands.

God had so ordered things that Jesus was selected to read from the scroll in the temple on that particular day. When the scribe handed him the book, the greatest book ever written, Jesus turned to the page where his very own divine purpose was outlined. Whether Jesus chose the passage from Isaiah 61:1-2 or whether it was the text printed in the daily bulletin is unknown to us.

What we do know is the Lord had anointed him for ministry. God had not anointed him with oil or the laying on of hands, the 'Spirit' of the Lord was on him! It was on him when he went into the wilderness. It was on him when he came out of the wilderness. It was on him when he entered that synagogue and it would be on him when he walked away from that phase of his ministry to fulfill his divine purpose.

Some of us anoint ourselves for the ministry. Dad was a preacher or Mama is a preacher, I want to be like him/her. "Oh, all pastors have to do is write sermons and sometimes visit the sick; I can do that." My brothers and my sisters do not be deceived. There is more to ministry than standing up before a congregation and saying, "Thus said the Lord." People are hurting. People are dying psychologically, physiologically, economically, socially and spiritually. They need anointed, appointed, and trained physicians to help them.

If you are not spiritually connected to and spiritually protected by God, the world will swallow you up like a bloody piece of meat in a hungry shark tank. Or they will send you out of the church disillusioned and running for your life. The Bible teaches us that when God calls you to a ministry and the people where you are don't accept you, God will send you to another place where God wants you to glorify the Lord.[152] Jesus was called first to the Jews, then to the Gentiles. Paul was also a Jew but he had to take his message and his ministry to the Gentiles.

However, before you can be sent out by God, you should know your divine purpose. What gifts do you possess? Who has God called you to serve? What service are you to render? Jesus knew his mission and his ministry. He was to proclaim or teach the Good News. What was this good news? Jesus was to proclaim salvation for the body, mind and spirit. Jesus was to proclaim liberation from sin and the penalty of sin. His proclamation was to offer freedom for those who were imprisoned, being held hostage by the forces of this world. He was to proclaim recovery of sight for those who were blind and could not find their way.

And Jesus was to declare release for those who were being oppressed by life and all of its consequences.

This was not to happen at the end of any holy war. It would not take place at some future point in time. Right now was the acceptable time! Right now was the acceptable time for Jesus to bring healing, restoration, and resurrection to the people of God. Right now was the acceptable time for somebody to be healed from demon possession. Right now was the acceptable time for somebody to have their sight restored. Right now was the acceptable time for somebody to be raised from the dead.

Are there any demon possessed Marys in the house? Those who struggle with emotional and psychological problems, addictions and obsessions. Are there any Blind Bartimaeuses in the house? Those who keep bumping their heads and stomping their feet over the same foolishness day in and day out. Are there any Lazaruses in the house? Those whose joy and praise have been locked up so long, there is no sign of life in you. Are you ready to be healed? Are you ready to be set free? Just, hold on – Your help is on the way! God is going to give you an opportunity to be healed!

As fate would have it, Jesus' ministry was not to be carried out in that synagogue, not in that church house. A prophet is not always fully accepted in his own country. And I would add, if the church already has a healer, if someone is already serving in the ministry that you have been called to perform. You are in the wrong place. Yes, that may be your church home; it may very well be your worship station. But it may not be your working place. It may not be your place of service or your place of full-time employment in the ministry. So, lift up your head. Straighten up your face. Stand tall and seek God's will and seek God's Under Servant's (your pastor's) blessing and move out into the mission field! Jesus said it himself, "The harvest is plentiful and the workers are few. Ask the Lord of the harvest, therefore, to send out workers into his harvest field."[153]

The scriptures tell us that initially the people were happy for Jesus. They were amazed at the gracious words that fell from his lips. When your anointing is fresh everybody will praise you. The people will usher you on. Don't get caught up in vain glory. After Jesus told them about the implications of his calling, they turned on him and ran him out of that community. But Jesus had on 'traveling shoes' so he walked away without harm or any ill effects of the experiences in his home town.

Among Jesus' many ministry gifts was evangelism, carrying the good news far and wide. And now was the acceptable time for Jesus to move forward with the ministry God had assigned to his hands. Jesus placed his full trust in God. So he marched on – he went forward in faith – he followed his destiny and the rest is history.

One Sunday morning following a forty-day sabbatical from my home church, God placed these thoughts in my spirit. Why is your spirit so restless and disquieted there? What is good about being where you are? What is it that you want to do in the church? What is it that I have called you to do? As I gave thought to each of these questions, my life and ministry over the past few years began to fast forward before my eyes. I took note of the blessings and the missed opportunities. God had opened doors for me to leave my home state to be employed in full time ministry and I did not go. I took note of the accomplishments and the mistakes that I had made. In spite of me being my own stumbling block, failing to go when sent out by the Lord, God opened other windows of opportunity for me to do volunteer work in diverse ministry settings. God continued to utilize my gifts for divine purposes.

In humble submission, I began to cry out to the Lord. Fear and doubt began to overwhelm me. The devil tried to hold me down. When God picked me up off the floor, my spirit was no longer downcast. The devil wanted to keep me in the wilderness; but God had set me free! I was excited. My knees started pumping and my hands started flying. My burdens had been lifted. I was ready to run on to see what the end was going to be.

When you trust God's spirit, it is good to search God's word and to find some scriptures that give meaning to your spiritual life and meaning to what God has called you to do. That's what Jesus did. The Isaiah passage was the scripture that most suited his divine purpose. Listen to it again: "The Lord has put his Spirit in me, because he appointed me to tell the good news to the poor. He has sent me to tell the captives they are free and to tell the blind that they can see again. God sent me to free those who have been treated unfairly and to announce the time when the Lord will show his kindness toward them."[154]

As for me, I have four passages of scripture that give me strength and move me forward.

1. Proverbs 3:5-6 reminds me that I am to trust in God. Therefore, I no longer try to rationalize every step I take. I simply live my life with godly integrity and allow the Lord to order my steps.

2. Jeremiah 29:11 reminds me that God has a divine plan for my life. God may not reveal it to me all at one time, but I know God's plan is not going to cause me harm. It will help me. This full reliance on God is what gives me hope for a brighter future.

3. When God called me into the ministry, I did not move forward with blinders on. I knew that Satan was going to come after me. I also knew that I would have some dark nights of the soul, when I would feel isolated and alone. But the 23rd Psalm reminds me that in my darkest hours God has not forsaken me. God takes my hand in quiet times. Following periods of prayer, fasting and rest, I am revived and my spirit is refreshed. The Lord is my guide. God makes his will known to me so that I can be faithful in service. When danger comes my way, as it so often has, God is with me. I am protected and unafraid. I am able to walk away unharmed. God supplies my every need. I am able to bask in the overflow of the Lord's anointing.

4. Luke 4:18-19 ~ I know that the Spirit of the Lord is upon me! I have been anointed and appointed to preach the Good News. I have been anointed and appointed to teach God's people how to rise above life's adversities. I have been anointed and appointed to empower God's people for service. And, I am ready to reach out and touch somebody for Jesus. It is God's Spirit that ushers me on!

That's why today I claim my divine purpose. Yes, now is my acceptable time. So I don't worry about what folks may say. It was Mark Twain who said, "A lie will go all the way around the world before the truth can get its shoes on." I am no longer concerned about my future. My future is in God's hands. I know that God wants me to go where God sends me. And I am so happy about it, I just want to celebrate. This is the year of the Lord's favor. God is ready to do some things through me and in me that God has not done before.

What about you? Are you uncomfortable living a life of sin? Is life slapping you on one side of your head and then the other? Do you feel as if you are spinning your wheels and getting nowhere fast?

Or, have you been set up by God? Has God's Spirit spoken to your spirit? Do you feel that the Lord is calling your name? Is the Holy Spirit telling you it's time to move on to a better life? Do you feel that God has an anointing on your life? Do you feel that God is calling you to serve in some capacity in the ministry? Or is it that God just wants you to come home, come into the household of faith?

Well, I've got some good news for you. Jesus is offering you forgiveness and acceptance. Jesus is offering you freedom and security. Jesus is offering you strength and a divine purpose for your life. Jesus is offering you hope and a future. Jesus is offering you joy and happiness. Jesus is offering you brighter days ahead.

Won't you trust him! Won't you surrender your life to him! Won't you allow the Lord to order your steps? Won't you let Jesus lead you? All the way from earth to heaven, let Jesus lead you all the way. Trust the unction of the Holy Spirit. Why don't you stand on your feet and just shout to God. Lord, I am ready. I'm ready. I'm ready! Use me, Lord. Use me, Lord. Use me, Lord! I am available. I'm available. I'm available. Lord, I am available to you. Use me Lord!

Now is your acceptable time. Trust God. Allow God to heal you. Allow God to make you whole. Allow God to lead you. Allow God to use you. Now is the Acceptable Time!

The doors of God's church are open. Man, Woman, Boy or Girl, if the Lord is whispering in your ears, I need you; I have a job for you. I want to give you freedom; I want to give you peace. Won't you come! If you are ready for God to take control of your life and bring you out of the wilderness and under God's arm of protection, won't you come forth! If you simply want to find your place of service in God's ministry won't you come! If you are a sinner in need of forgiveness, won't you come! The doors are open wide; now is your acceptable time! Won't you come to Jesus!

If you are reading this book, go to a church where you feel the presence of the Lord inviting you to live out your divine calling. If you are already a member of a church, and you are at peace there, meet with a ministry leader or your pastor and begin living out your divine purpose through renewed commitment to service.

God had given this sermon title to me, years ago. I had tried to write a sermon on this text. My previous attempts were futile. I had missed God's implications for this text in my own ministry. But, this time God wrote the sermon and I simply lived it out. When God takes you back to the same place where you have found yourself before, stop, inquire of God and then follow the dictates of the Holy Spirit. Halleluiah, Thank you, Jesus! I am on my way...Amen.

A Servant on the Way...living out God's divine purposes in this present age!
The Reverend Evaleen Litman Talton Sargent

About the Author

"But you will receive power when the Holy Spirit comes on you; and you will be my witnesses in Jerusalem, and in all Judea and Samaria, and to the ends of the earth."~ Acts 1:8

Reverend Evaleen Litman Sargent is an ordained Gospel preacher. She serves God's people as a teacher, workshop facilitator, short-term missionary and Christian counselor. A quiet and humble spirit, she confessed Christ as her Lord and Savior at the age of twelve. As a youth, she was called to preach but circumstances in our society prevented her from fully sharing her gifts. Realizing that God is the giver of all gifts and that God will set up divine appointments for the utilization of the *Gifts of the Spirit*, Rev. Sargent willing serves in the areas of her calling.

God refreshed her call to the ministry in 1993 and on January 19, 1994, she was licensed to preach the gospel by the Mt. Calvary Baptist Church. In August 1997, she founded *ELS Ministries* whose mission is to empower persons to go into all settings continuing Christ's ministry of healing and restoration to a broken people (Luke 4:18-19).

Sargent graduated valedictorian from Carver School of Nursing and attended Georgia State University. She completed her seminary degree in May 2000 at the Morehouse School of Religion, Interdenominational Theological Center, Inc. (ITC), graduating Summa Cum Laude in the top 5% of her class, with a Master of Divinity Degree in Church Administration and Pastoral Care and Counseling. After graduation, bent, but not broken, Rev. Sargent took a wilderness sabbatical spending time with the Lord and seeking healing, restoration and renewal.

She was ordained to preach the gospel on February 11, 2001 by the Lindsay Street Baptist Church. Under the unction of the Holy Spirit, she founded *The POWER OF GOD* Conference: The Woman in the Mirror, a healing and transformation retreat. In 2002, she founded The Mission Institute and "Your Choice" Center, Inc., a faith-based non-profit community development corporation specializing in social service ministries that empower persons with life skills training for self-sufficiency.

Sargent is the recipient of a Lilly Foundation grant through the Institute for Clergy Excellence to travel and study preaching and worship leadership across the United States and internationally. Rev. Sargent is a certified facilitator for "Nurturing God's Way Parenting Program" and a Girl Scouts of America volunteer. She is on the Board of Education and Publication for the Progressive National Baptist Convention, Inc. She is also a life member of the Georgia Association and the National Association of Minister's Wives and Minister's Widows, Inc. This woman of God is an author with sermons published in the African American Pulpit and devotionals published in numerous publications including *Women at the Well*, Vol. 2. Her own book, *Extraordinary Women: Helping a Sister Out* was published in 2007.

Previously, she has served as Program Director for Church and Community, Urban Theological Institute (UTI) at the Interdenominational Theological Center, Inc. (ITC), Dean of the New Era Congress of Christian Education, and Director of Programming for the New Era Missionary Baptist Convention of Georgia, Inc. and Edward R. Davie Missions Conference. She has traveled as a short-term missionary to Africa, Jamaica and Haiti. Rev. Sargent was also an Accredited Visitor to the Eighth Annual Assembly of the

World Council of Churches in Harare, Zimbabwe. She was Chairman of Personal Development for American Baptist Women of the South, Area III and the Minister in Residence for the 2002 Orientation to ABC Life Conference in Wisconsin for the American Baptist Churches, USA. Sargent has had distinguished careers in the auto industry, communications, nursing, banking, and mortgage lending being the first black female to attain many of the positions she has held. She has served on the board of directors for local and national businesses and organizations.

Rev. Evaleen understands that God doesn't use her because she's the Lord's only option. She is in awe of the tremendous privilege that God gives, inviting her and each of us to be a witness of God's glorious power. Rev. Sargent is well aware of the fact that God does not intend for us to share the gospel under our own strength. God enables us, through the Holy Spirit, to have a part in the divine purpose of drawing people to the Creator and Lord. God's Spirit prompts us to spread the good news. God's Spirit fills us with power and we see amazing things happen when we obey God's prompting. Rev. Sargent strives to be sensitive to the ways the Spirit of God leads her, and trusts that the Lord will empower her with wisdom to always obey God's leading. As she witnesses daily out of her own life experiences, Sargent is a willing vessel in the Potter's hands, referring to herself as *"A Servant on the Way...living out God's divine purpose in this present age!"*

She is the widow of the Reverend Dr. Charles J. Sargent, a former pastor and seminary professor. Her heart lights up her face as she shares her love for her sons, the Rev. Delvin D. Talton, Sr., and the Rev. James E. Talton II, Associate Ministers, Dixie Hills First Baptist Church; her daughter in-law, Sheila owner of God's Little Angels Day

Care; and three precious grandchildren: Jamil Evaleen, Delvin, Jr., and Maya, who loving call her 'Big Mama.' Her motto is "Try God, Trust God and See" (Proverbs 3:5-6); favorite poem, *"Still I Rise"* by Maya Angelou and her theme song is *"I Trust in God."*

Bibliography

Broadman Biblical Commentary. Revised ed., volume 1. Nashville: Broadman Press, 1973.

Broadman Biblical Commentary. Revised ed., volume 2. Nashville: Broadman Press, 1970.

Brown, Raymond E., Joseph A. Fitzmyer, and Roland E. Murphy. The New Jerome Biblical Commentary. Englewood Cliff, NJ: Prentice-Hall, 1990.

Davis, Nanette J., ed. *Prostitution: An International Handbook on Trends, Problems, and Policies.* Westport, CT: Greenwood Press, 1993.

Hunter, Rodney J., Ed. *Dictionary of Pastoral Care and Counseling.* Nashville: Abingdon Press, 1990.

Keil, C. F. and F. Delitzsch. *Commentary on the Old Testament.* Peabody, MA: Hendrickson Publishers, 1996.

McKim, Donald K., ed. *Westminster Dictionary of Theological Terms.* Louisville: Westminster John Knox Press, 1996.

Ryken, Leland, James C. Wilhoit, and Tremper Longman, III. *Dictionary of Biblical Imagery.* Downers Grove, IL: InterVarsity Press, 1998.

Word Biblical Commentary. Waco, TX: Word Books, 1983.

References

1 1 Corinthians 1:17.

2 Isaiah 52:15; Romans 15:21.

3 *Word Biblical Commentary*, volume 35a, 412 and 419.

4 Luke 10:40b.

5 Luke 10:40c.

6 John 12:2.

7 1 Peter 4:9-10.

8 Charles V. Bryant, *Rediscovering Our Spiritual Gifts* (Nashville: Upper Room Books, 1991), 94.

9 John 11:5.

10 John 11:20-22.

11 John 11:28.

12 1 Peter 3:13-18.

13 *Dictionary of Pastoral Care and Counseling,* 438.

14 *Dictionary of Pastoral Care and Counseling*, 358.

15 According to the United States Census Bureau 2000 date, the ratio of non-institutionalized unmarried men per 100 unmarried women is 86% for the United States and Puerto Rico. State of Georgia statistics are the same, released October 23, 2003. However, when we consider the fact that in a large number of states across the United States, African-American men are incarcerated at a much higher rate for the same crimes as other races of men; the ratio of African-American men who are available for marriage per 100 African-American single women would be much lower.

16 *Webster's Ninth New Collegiate Dictionary*, s. v. "Passion." *Dictionary of Pastoral Care and Counseling*, s. v. "Emotion." Passion in the sense we use it here is an intense, driving, overmastering feeling or conviction. It is synonymous with fervor, ardor, enthusiasm or zeal. It is an intense emotion, compelling action, deeply stirring the soul. Passion is a strong liking or desire for or devotion to some person, activity, object or concept directed by the Holy Spirit.

17 Luke 10:39-42.

18 John 11:3-20.

[19] John 11:28-44.

[20] John 12:1-8.

[21] Matthew 27:55; Mark 15:40-41; Luke 23:27-28,49.

[22] Acts 1:14; 2:14-18.

[23] Psalm 100:4-5.

[24] Quenching the Spirit is a way of maintaining self-control for many of us. In a pastoral counseling class with Dr. Carolyn McCrary at the Interdenominational Theological Center (ITC), I learned that I was also cutting off my emotional responses to stressful conditions in my life. Sometimes yielding in the 'shout' can open the door to your breakthrough in other areas.

[25] *Dictionary of Pastoral Care and Counseling*, s. v. "Psychopathology and Religion," 1014.

[26] Matthew 28:18-20.

[27] Luke 4:17-21: And the scroll of the prophet Isaiah was given to him. He unrolled the scroll and found the place where it was written: "The Spirit of the Lord is upon me, because he has anointed me to bring good news to the poor. He has sent me to proclaim release to the captives and recovery of sight to the blind, to let the oppressed go free, to proclaim the year of the Lord's favor"...Then he began to say to them, "Today this scripture has been fulfilled in your hearing."

[28] John 12:26.

[29] 2 Corinthians 3:17.

[30] T. R. Hobbs, *Word Biblical Commentary, 2 Kings,* volume 13, 103.

[31] Raymond B. Dilliard, *Word Biblical Commentary, 2 Chronicles,* volume 15, 176-177.

[32] 2 Kings 11:1-3; 2 Chronicles 22:10-12.

[33] 2 Kings 11:4-16.

[34] Raymond B. Dilliard, *Word Biblical Commentary, 2 Chronicles,* volume 15, 176-177.

[35] T. R. Hobbs, *Word Biblical Commentary, 2 Kings,* volume 13, 142-143.

[36] 2 Chronicles 23:1-15.

[37] 1 Kings 19:1-16.

[38] *Dictionary of Pastoral Care and Counseling*, s. v. "Family Theory and Therapy," 425.

[39] Parties where a fee is sometimes paid for entrance and the entertainment is women and/or men performing erotic dancing and perverted sex acts with one or multiple partners in exchange for drugs and sometimes money.

[40] Proverbs 19:21.

[41] Taken from an insert in "Our Daily Bread" mailer in August 2003.

[42] Proverbs 3:5-6.

[43] Matthew 11:28-30.

[44] Matthew 6:10b.

[45] 1 Corinthians 2:12-3:6.

[46] Judges 4:17-24.

[47] *Jerome Biblical Commentary*, 133-34.

[48] *Broadman Biblical Commentary*, 403-412.

[49] Matthew 7:7

[50] Esther 4:16; 8:5-8

[51] Deuteronomy 32:48-52; 34:1-4

[52] 2 Corinthians 12:7a-10

[53] 1 Kings 3:9-13

[54] 1 John 5:14

[55] 1 Chronicles 17

[56] Ephesians 4:7

[57] Ephesians 4:11-12

[58] I have developed a workshop and sermon built around this theme.

[59] Exodus 17:12.

[60] I have developed a workshop on spiritually gifted armor bearers.

[61] 1 Thessalonians 5:12.

[62] Romans 12:16-17.

[63] Psalm 34:1-2

[64] Although God provided a ram to replace Isaac on the altar, both stories involved a father offering his child as a blood sacrifice to the Lord.

[65] Judges 11:1-11.

[66] Judges 11:9-28.

[67] Judges 11:29.

[68] C. F. Keil and F. Delitzsch, *Commentary on the Old Testament*, volume 2. (Peabody, MA: Hendrickson Publishers, Inc., 1996).

[69] Judges 11:35.

[70] *Dictionary of Biblical Imagery*, s. v. "Vows, Oaths."

[71] Judges 11:36.

[72] Judges 11:37-40.

[73] *Dictionary of Biblical Imagery*, s. v. "Vows, Oaths."

[74] Deuteronomy 23:21-23; Proverbs 20:25.

[75] Exodus 20:7; Deuteronomy 5:11.

[76] 1 Peter 1:6-7.

[77] This sermon was first preached at the Mt. Calvary Baptist Church in Atlanta, Georgia in August 1999. It was later published in the Fall 2000 Seminarians' Issue of *The African American Pulpit*. It is used here with permission of Judson Press.

[78] John 5:8 NKJV.

[79] Luke 6:22, NRSV.

[80] Luke 6:22-23, *The Message*.

[81] Mark 5:30; Luke 8:47.

[82] *Word Biblical Commentary*, volume 35a, 420.

[83] Luke 8:47.

[84] Isaiah 53:5

[85] Brochures are available on line at *www.pueblo.gsa.gov* or you may write U.S. Department of Agriculture, Center for Nutrition Policy and Promotion, 1120 20th St., NW, Suite 200, North Lobby, Washington, DC 20036-3475.

[86] *www.voiceofwomen.com.*

[87] Hot flashes are the result of blood vessels irregularly dilating and constricting.

[88] Menstruation is a discharging of blood, secretions, and tissue debris from the uterus that occurs in women at monthly intervals and is considered to be a readjustment of the uterus to the non-pregnant state following changes resulting from ovulation.

[89] *Dictionary of Pastoral Care and Counseling*, s. v. "Menopause," 708-9. Some women suffer from pre-menopausal syndrome, the cessation of menstruation accompanied by a combination of physical, psychological and/or changes in behavior of sufficient severity to

result in deterioration in interpersonal relationships and the interference of normal activities.

90 *Dictionary of Pastoral Care and Counseling*, s. v. "Spiritual Depression," 1103-6. Spiritual Depression is a condition in which life on all fronts seems to be blocked. Often it directs our attention to a way or style of life that needs to be changed. It is often referred to as a wilderness journey. You are in a desert place lonely and without the water of life; however, it is a place where angels can minister and distraught persons can find transformation.

91 Matthew 3:17.

92 Matthew 8:17.

93 Acts 9:36.

94 Acts 9:39.

95 Matthew 25:35-36.

96 Acts 9:40.

97 Psalm 116:15.

98 Baptism is a death-rebirth ritual. As the believer is buried with Christ by baptism into death, as Christ was raised from the dead by God, we too can walk in newness of life. Romans 6:4.

99 Regeneration is to be born again. To leave the death of sin and live a Christ-like life. John 3:1-8.

100 Acts 9:41-42.

101 Acts 9:42.

102 Philippians 2:1-5, 8.

103 *Dictionary of Biblical Imagery*, 676-678.

104 Hosea 9:1.

105 This may have been the same one used for their later escape from the city.

106 *Word Biblical Commentary*, 68-69.

107 C. F. Keil and F. Delitzsch, *Biblical Commentary*, 49-53.

108 Matthew 1:5-16.

109 *The New Jerome Biblical Commentary*, 117.

110 Hebrews 11:31.

111 James 2:25.

112 www.wmich.edu/~destiny/statistics.htm.

[113] Nanette J. Davis, ed., *Prostitution: An International Handbook on Trends, Problems, and Policies,* 1993.

[114] Acts 16:14; 40; 17:4; 12.

[115] Hebrews 11:6.

[116] Matthew 6:8.

[117] Philippians 4:8-9.

[118] Luke 8:1-2.

[119] John 10:26; Luke 8:26-29; Luke 13:11, 16; Revelation 16:14.

[120] Persons in the church seeking care and counseling for what is believed to be demon possession should be firmly but compassionately referred to competent psychiatric agencies for evaluation and treatment. However, their deep spiritual needs should not be overlooked during the referral process. Although we want to sentence the demon-possessed person to death who molests a child, robbing them of their innocence and distorting their vision of God, we must also pray for their soul.

[121] Matthew 12.28.

[122] Luke 4:19-19; John 12:27-32.

[123] Luke 8:3.

[124] John 19:25.

[125] Mark 15:37.

[126] Matthew 27:61; Mark 15:47.

[127] Matthew 28:1-10; Mark 16:1-9; Luke 24:1-12.

[128] Matthew 28:9; John 20:1-18.

[129] Mark 28:10.

[130] Ephesians 4:11-12.

[131] 1 Thessalonians 5:12-13.

[132] Galatians 6:4; Philippians 4:9.

[133] 2 Timothy 3:10-14.

[134] 2 Thessalonians 3:1.

[135] Genesis 2:9-20.

[136] *Westminster Dictionary of Theological Terms,* 286. That which is passed on from one to another.

[137] Genesis 3:1-6.

[138] 1 Corinthians 2:12; *Westminster Dictionary of Theological Terms,* 266.

[139] Genesis 3:14-19.

[140] Raymond B. Dilliard, *Word Biblical Commentary*, Genesis, volume 1, 78-86.

[141] *Word Biblical Commentary*, volume 1, 116

[142] C. F. Keil and F. Delitzsch, volume 1, 63.

[143] Note: I would like to thank my son, Rev. James Talton, for encouraging me to watch the movie and my daughter-in-law, Minister Ericia Talton for providing the DVD.

[144] 2 Corinthians 11:3

[145] Romans 3:23.

[146] Romans 6:12.

[147] *Dictionary of Pastoral Care and Counseling*, 1162.

[148] Romans 10:9.

[149] C. Austin Miles, "In the Garden" (Hall-Mack Co., 1912, Renewed 1940, The Rodeheaver Co., Owner).

[150] Romans 8:26-30.

[151] Jesus was born in Bethlehem and spent his youth in Nazareth.

[152] Luke 10:13-15; Romans 9-11.

[153] Matthew 9:37-38.

[154] Luke 4:18-19 NCV.